T0266994

PRAISE FOR
A WAR AWAY...

Tess Johnston clearly had the time of her life as a gutsy young staffer at the hub of US operations in South Vietnam. In this breezy memoir, she relates tales of dating pilots, hitching lifts around the Delta by chopper, and occasionally getting shot at or dodging mortar shells. Her narrative conveys the addictive buzz of discovery familiar to many Westerners in Asia, intensified by a devastating war.
— Christopher MacDonald, author of *The Science of War*

A riveting memoir of a Southern belle doing her bit to fight the war in Vietnam. Johnston gives a deeply personal and frank account of the highlights and low points of her life as a "Round Eye" girl in a country at war. Her openness and eye for detail make you feel you lived in country - including surviving the Tet Offensive and the death of a lover - with her . I recommended it highly.
— Douglas Clark, author or *Justice by Gunboat*

A gripping memoir of Tess Johnston's seven years "on the ground" during the Vietnam War. A genteel Southern belle, Tess opted for the road (much) less traveled and her account of the following seven years of living and working in Vietnam is fascinating, sometimes ribald and always fascinating.
— Joseph Borich, former US Consul General, Shanghai

Tess Johnston is known to many as an American denizen of Shanghai, but she has a Vietnam story that has long been waiting to be told and it is a great read. Much has been written about the Vietnam war (or the American War as they call it here), but almost none of it from the perspective of an American woman.
— Fred Burke, long-term American resident of Saigon

A WAR AWAY

An American Woman in Vietnam, 1967-1974

Tess Johnston

A War Away

By Tess Johnston

ISBN-13: 978-988-8422-86-9

Cover design: Jason Wong

Photos: All photographs were taken by Tess Johnston, except those depicting her which were taken by various boyfriends.

HISTORY / Asia / Vietnam

EB105

Published by Earnshaw Books Ltd. (Hong Kong)

Contents

"It's all about being in the right place at the right (or wrong) time."

FOREWORD

MOST OF THE VIETNAM stories that follow were written in a white heat of creativity that hit me in the first two years after I returned from Vietnam late in 1974. In writing that book, I felt I had a story to share: what it was like to be a young female in a combat zone. My experiences were perhaps not unique – but how many women lived there for seven years during the war and then recorded it?

In 2017, upon my repatriation to the United States, I found a box containing an early draft of a book I had totally forgotten about: my seven years in Vietnam. The narrative from that manuscript attempted to show what it was like being in such an historically interesting and challenging place and time.

My time in Vietnam plus my later China years brings me up to a total of 43 years in Asia – now exactly half my lifetime. And as a confessed 'Adrenalin Junkie,' my five tours in Vietnam were the most exciting years of my life, by the sheer luck of being in the right place and at the right (some might say wrong) time. War is invigorating – if you don't get killed or wounded in it. As my previous memoir covered Shanghai, now I can end my personal saga with this story from forty years ago, in a far away war.

CAVEATS: Much of the draft of this book was written long ago. If Vietnam veterans read this and find discrepancies, I can only say that at the time many portions were written, it represented my still-vivid memories of events. I have changed all of the names to protect the privacy of all the individuals other than Vann, Wilson, Weyand and Frenchy (now all long gone).

Tess Johnston
Washington, DC
January 2018

1

SAIGON

IN THE SUMMER of 1967 after several years of teaching German at Virginia colleges, I had become bored with the routine and I asked for, and was granted, a year off to decide if I wanted to continue that career path. A friend then told me of an urgent call for secretaries to work in Vietnam for USAID, the US Agency for International Development, and we both decided to apply. She later got cold feet, but I went anyway. (My one year ultimately stretched into seven – and thus my career choice decision became moot.) Why not? We were needed in Vietnam, the pay was high, the tour was for only eighteen months and it sounded exciting. I applied and was immediately accepted – indicating how desperate was their need. I went to Washington for my six weeks of Vietnamese language classes before flying to Saigon. In class, I sat beside a lively gal who had quite a plum New York City job. She was funny, adventurous, and we liked each other from the start. We talked about going to Vietnam, wondering if it was the right move.

"You wanted to go that far away?" I asked. "A war away?"

"Sure!" she replied.

It turned out that she was to depart for Saigon about the same time as I. We coordinated and agreed that we should take the same flight, using our authorized rest day in exotic Hong Kong

rather than the more prosaic Hawaii. We did so for three dyna-
mite days.

Hong Kong in September of 1967 was an electrifying city,
crowded, sweaty, bustling, beautiful, the modern and the ancient, the sleek and the grubby, all tossed into one big pulsating
jumble. It was our first taste of Asia and we loved it. In those
early days the harbor was still wide and little motorboats called
wallah-wallahs, scuttling like water bugs, carried us back from
the shopping delights of Kowloon side to deposit us just below
our elegant hotel, the old Hilton so beloved by expats, now gone
and replaced by a boring modern building. We would then take
the cog railway up the green hills to Victoria Peak and drink
fresh-squeezed lemonade in the garden of a little English tea
room. There we would cool off as the city and the wide blue water shimmered below us.

We did the popular bus tour to the New Territories that bor-
dered on China and stared through binoculars to get a closer
view of that forbidden, closed country. All we saw of it was a
vast spread of rice paddies and peasants in conical hats walking behind their water buffaloes. This mysterious "Red" China
turned out to be tranquil and bright green. If only we had known!
The country was just then moving into the so-called "Cultural
Revolution" that was to tear it apart for the next decade. And
what we saw then has now become a sprawling urban-industrial
complex, a city called Shenzhen, all high-rises and asphalt with
little green to be seen anywhere.

We had utilized the trick of taking our rest days over a weekend, thus stretching them to four, but all too soon this busy "rest"
interlude was over. We repacked our now-bulging bags and flew
off to our new life in Saigon. The city lay about a thousand miles
south of Hong Kong and we slept for the first hour over the water. But when the cabin pressure changed and stewardesses be-

gan to bustle, we perked up to peer out the window. Looking down on Vietnam was a bit like looking into China from Hong Kong through binoculars. Below us, the landscape was again one of lush green fields, now laced with winding waterways and small creeks. Then finally we saw a sprawling white city of low buildings bordering a broad, brown river filled with sampans and ships of all sizes. This was to be our new 'home town'.

Saigon's old airport, Tan Son Nhut, was no longer a peacetime one. The low whitewashed terminal building that had served the French in their colonization of Indo-China was now the terminal of an air base used jointly by both the USAF and VNAF (US and Vietnam Air Forces). It was surrounded by barbed wire fencing, dotted with machine gun towers and filled with Quonset huts, sandbagged revetments and military aircraft lining its runways.

The airport was a busy place, and the airline on which we flew just wanted to get in and out of there as fast as it could. There were no frills to the ground services and the manual unloading of luggage was the fastest I had ever seen. In the terminal, our minders met us and then shepherded us through, slapping our papers first on Vietnamese and then on American counters. Our luggage miraculously appeared out of the chaos and in probably less than twenty minutes we were loaded, along with other dazed official travelers, into an olive-green military bus.

Soon we were driving down Cong Ly, the main road from the airport, amidst a gaggle of jeeps, cars, motorbikes, bicycles, pedicabs, and just about every other form of locomotion you can think of. They all wove in and out, crossed and recrossed, swerved and overtook, and all honked without ceasing. Yet somehow it all continued flowing in a current of multiple but cohesive waves that somehow swept us into Saigon's hotel and business center. It was a heart-stopping – and predictive – ride.

There were three major hotels clustered along the broad bou-

3

levards: the Continental, preferred by the French; the Caravelle, preferred by the correspondents; and the all-military Rex. A little farther along were a series of smaller, narrow hotels of five to ten storeys, all now filled with USAID staffers. One, the Oscar Hotel, was to be our new home. Our first night there was spent in a room without windows. Because of the narrow street frontage and buildings on both sides, the hotel had outside windows only on the higher floors and at the front and back of the hotel. The dark interior had "courtyards" – actually just enlarged air shafts open to the sky to admit some light and to disperse the fetid air spewed out by the air conditioners in all the rooms around these light wells.

These small rooms were basically just stacked concrete shelves, each with its own tiny concrete bathroom. The only wood in the room, aside from the headboards and slats of the hard beds, was the warped door of a small closet and a chest with sticking drawers.

And this ugly utilitarian cave was to be my home for the indefinite future?! My heart sank.

The next morning, Sally and I talked over breakfast as we waited for transportation to USAID headquarters for our job assignments. Sally was very chatty and social and she had already found out that if we would agree to share a room, we could have one of the front ones – with windows! She was a small, blond, freckled and feisty, and I am sure that she dazzled the room clerk to get us that coveted room assignment, for which I will owe her until my dying day.

I had no idea how USAID's job assignments were made, but it didn't matter because as Newbies we were going to get the worst ones – that you could count on. Sally went to an office in the Mondial Hotel, which sounded terribly continental and much better than mine. Time has mercifully drawn a veil over my job.

I recall only being in a typing pool in a vertical concrete slab of a building in a less attractive suburb. I was rapidly beginning to regret my impulsive decision to come to the exotic East to watch a war. This was not exotic at all; it was in fact pretty grotty. But there was a war on and I am not a whiner, so I decided to pull up my socks and get on with it, work hard and hope for better days. Which were soon to come.

After our first day at work – Sally's job turned out to be only a step above my dreary one – she and I speedily moved into our new room, before someone could take it away from us; we were definitely too low-ranking to merit it. Our new and improved room was broad, half the width of the building, and considerably larger than our previous one. The front had two large barred windows that let in light. They even let in air when we opened them, but with the steamy heat and the unceasing racket and exhaust fumes from the hectic traffic below, we seldom did.

A door from the hotel corridor was at the center of the room so Sally took one half and I the other. We pushed and shoved our two large free-standing wardrobes side by side to form a sort of room divider, providing us a bit of privacy. We could not see each other's beds but we could clearly hear everything that went on in the room. Not an ideal arrangement but we luckily would not be spending a lot of time there. Although lacking a lot, our new and utilitarian shared room was a vast improvement over the one in which we had spent our first night. Things were already looking up.

We soon discovered the recessed open terrace of Saigon's colonial gem, the famed Continental Hotel of Graham Greene and other authors. It was called the Continental Shelf by its regulars, who consisted of everyone from French rubber planters down for the weekend to the randy roving officers of several nations. Under slow ceiling fans, elderly Vietnamese waiters moved among the tables, indifferent to us but obsequious to the French. You could linger for hours over an exotic long drink or a refreshing citron pressé made from local limes.

On the street just beyond the flower boxes were pimps and prostitutes, beggars and hustlers. There were also vendors of everything imaginable from fragrant jasmine sold by old ladies and children to whispered offerings – dope? condoms? their sisters? – from dodgy-looking local males. We found it far more comfortable and exotic than sitting on the Rex's tiled rooftop filled with drunken GIs and their Vietnamese girlfriends. The Continental was run by French-Vietnamese and was more expensive than the military-run Rex so it attracted a higher clientele, or so we fancied.

Usually we had hardly sat down before drinks or flowers would appear at our table, sometimes sent over with a note, or along with men, officers or civilians, who asked if they could sit and talk to us. If we liked their looks they could; if they were drunk or not our type we explained we were waiting for our friends, implying male ones, as they usually were. We might move on later with our escorts to dinner somewhere, to noisy nightclubs or maybe just stroll down to the river, past a flower market and the curbside food-sellers of all sorts.

Our favorite was always a 'soup kitchen' consisting of a brazier suspended at one end of a bamboo carrying-pole and a basket of bowls at the other. These mobile outfits offered the delicious *pho*, for which Vietnam is still famous. We would sit on small stools and watch as the cook, often an older Vietnamese woman, ladled the boiling broth over rice noodles, adding thin slices of beef – possibly buffalo? – and bean sprouts, then something green and leafy, and finally tossing a wedge of lime into the mix. We needed only add a squirt or two of *nuoc mam*, the local pungent fish sauce, and we had a feast for the gods. I salivate still, as I write about it.

I soon discovered that Sally was the ultimate party girl. A Big City Girl, she loved to drink and could hold prodigious quantities, while I could not drink worth a hoot and hated the taste of beer. Sally and I still got along fine as room-mates but we soon parted ways socially and led separate lives, mine far more sedate than hers. She was often out till very late at night and I got up earlier in the morning so we really did not see a lot of each other. (We still do not, but we remain good friends.)

In addition to the company of charming officers there were other evening pursuits. When the weather was not too steamy it was lovely being driven along the river in a *cyclopousse*. This was a bicycle rickshaw where the driver pedaled along behind the passenger who sat in a wide seat in front (thus becoming the bumper of the *cyclo*.) It had a retractable canopy, used mostly to shield passengers from the sun or rain so seldom used at night. One glided along under the stars with an open view in the front and only the subdued swish-swish of the pedaling behind.

Because of the passenger's exposed position – and being just inches from everything around – it was necessary to sit with your purse tucked in behind you on the seat. Otherwise purse-snatchers on mopeds could swing by, scoop it up with ease and be lost in the moving stream before you even knew what was happening. Foreign females were a favorite target as we carried more money. We also wore expensive wristwatches – a bonus – and snatchers would often attempt to grab them off our wrists. This was easier done when we later drove our cars. On hot days our left arms usually lay temptingly exposed on the car's door-sill. (My watch was almost snatched one day but luckily, when the strap snapped the watch dropped back into my lap and the thief quickly darted off to pursue his trade elsewhere.)

Often by soothing *cyclo* I began to go to evening events at the Vietnamese-American Association. The VAA held lectures by speakers ranging from military officers to experts on various facets of Vietnamese culture. It was one of these events that was to present me, out of the blue, with another fork in the road – a change to my life. Almost from the day I arrived in Saigon, I had heard the name John Paul Vann. The people I knew talked about him all the time; they either admired him or not but he was always in the news.

I learned that Vann had come to Vietnam in 1962 as a Lieutenant Colonel in the Army, but was now a civilian. He had risen to one of the highest ranks in CORDS or Civil Operations and Revolutionary Development Support (the "Revolutionary" was later modified to the more bland "Rural"). CORDS was an integrated operation that consisted of half military and half civilian advisors stationed in Vietnam's four military regions. These were always referred to by the number followed by "Corps": I (pronounced Eye) Corps was up north bordering on North Vietnam; II Corps was south of that in the highlands; III Corps consisted of the provinces around Saigon; and IV Corps was the Mekong Delta to the south.

When I arrived, Vann had been newly named as the DEP-CORDS (Deputy for CORDS) in III Corps with his headquarters some kilometers west of Saigon in Bien Hoa. It had a large air base and there was a huge, sprawling Army base nearby at Long Binh.

Vann was a controversial and colorful figure, outspoken to the point of recklessness, and thus the darling of the press corps because he was always good for a pithy quote; he knew what he was talking about, usually spot on. When asked by one of President Johnson's White House advisors if he thought that the war would be over in six months, Vann reportedly replied: "Oh, I think we can hold out longer than that."

Vann did not try to conceal his distaste for the "desk jockeys" safely ensconced in Saigon who had never been in the field nor heard a shot fired; he also had little use for the State Department in its role in the CORDS coalition. He was a larger-than-life character and a lightning rod for the competing camps with their own theories on how the war in Vietnam, then decades-old, should be fought and could be won. He reputedly knew just about everything there was to know about the country and its war. The fact that he was not hesitant to tell anyone this – including his bosses, numerous generals, and the press – made him either the most hated or the most respected man in Vietnam; certainly no one was indifferent to him.

When I saw the notice that Vann was going to be the speaker at the VAA, I knew this was one lecture I did not want to miss. I showed up early and luckily got a seat right up front, as the house soon became packed. Never having seen Vann, I had a vision in my mind of what he would look like: sort of John Wayne-ish, tall and definitely tough looking, as his uber-bravery was already legendary. Then onto the stage strode a short, tanned, and sharp-profiled man with a receding hairline. This was John Paul Vann?!

Two minutes after he started to speak there was no longer any doubt about it: this was The Man. Almost immediately, Vann had the audience in the palm of his hand. It was his rhetoric rather than his voice that did it. His voice was rather high-pitched with a "redneck" accent – no captivation factor there. He told us what the NVA was up to, namely that it was going to make its big move soon. He rattled off troop figures on both sides, orders of battle, the names of the NVA officers, those they would be facing on our side, and what we should do about it. As I recall, he also said – but named no names – that our side was dithering with indecision and that no one could yet agree on anything. Or do I

9

remember that only from hindsight?

Vann summed up, took no questions, said good-night and strode off stage. I thought he had been speaking for about fifteen minutes but my watch revealed he had been talking at machine-gun speed for nearly an hour. I think the audience was stunned, or maybe mesmerized, as I don't recall any applause. It had been a stellar performance and indeed, his less-than-impressive looks now forgotten, I was dazzled by the man – and by his message. I decided then and there that somehow I was going to work for him. Now all I had to do was figure out how to make that happen.

In Vietnam, changes of job were usually the result of personal contacts and a lot of spadework by the person wanting the change. I soon realized that as far as the Personnel Office was concerned, a warm body for a vacant slot was the only thing that mattered and any consideration of abilities or preferences was mostly lost in the shuffle. I began to lay the groundwork for a transfer out of Saigon to III Corps in Bien Hoa and to John Paul Vann.

My move turned out to be easier than I expected. I met someone who knew Vann and agreed to mention me to him. My interlocutor apparently outlined my Foreign Service tour a few years earlier in Berlin and said I was young and foolish and wanted to work in the field. Something in the spiel appealed to Vann and he agreed to meet with me on one of his quick trips to Saigon. After about two minutes of staccato questions, he must have liked my equally short answers and I was hired. A fortnight later, I said goodbye to Sally, who promised to come out often to visit me, and was happily out of Saigon and the Oscar Hotel and on my way to Vann's headquarters in Bien Hoa and to my new and more fulfilling life in the provinces – tenfold!

2

The Doctor

Mota is hunched over the steering wheel with a look of myopic concentration. I have had another fight with the Motor Pool over sending me off to unknown locations with drivers knowing even less than I do. But Mota assures me that he knows the street address printed on the medical consult form: it's a main thoroughfare in Cho Lon, the Chinese section of Saigon, and he is sure he can find it. After all, he is nicknamed Mota because no one can remember his real name and because he is one of the brighter lights in the Motor (he pronounced it, "Mota") Pool.

We're well into the five o'clock rush hour and the motor bikes and bicycles eddy and flow around us in intricately interwoven patterns. I alternately close my eyes and flinch at each impending disaster only to see it melt into fluidity just short of impact. I agree with my clever friends: the only remedy is to unfold your newspaper the moment you get in the back seat and never glance up from it until you reach your destination. But I am in the front seat and it's a Scout and not a sedan. From my lofty perch I can see every mind-boggling motor scooter, motor bike, motorcycle, bicycle, pedicab, jeep, sedan, truck, lorry, bus, and aimlessly wandering pedestrian, in ever-changing configurations in our path.

Gradually the wide boulevard of the more "elegant" section

of Saigon begins to meld into the teeming hurly-burly that characterizes the Chinese section – roughly two-thirds of this urban area. Both sides of the street are lined with shops that resemble bowling lanes: they consist of narrow openings, seldom more than eight to ten feet wide but stretching far back into the dim recesses where the family also lives and works. There is seldom a store front in any traditional sense with a display window or a doorway. The wares often spill out in front of the shop onto the sidewalk, sometimes to the curb and jutting out between parked Hondas, children playing, and the assorted impedimenta that make walking in Saigon so difficult. This is the real core of the business world of Saigon, not the one or two boulevards "downtown" that cater to Westerners and wealthy Vietnamese. Here, housewives searching for bargains, coolies, students, civil servants, wealthy Chinese all mix and mingle and overflow into the streets, dodging between the creeping cars and ubiquitous *cyclos* that are especially popular and practical in the narrow streets in this section of the city.

Occasionally the shops are clustered by specialty but mostly it's one of each in random repetition down the street, interspersed with soup shops and tea houses, their chairs and tables also spilling out into the streets. Almost everything is represented, from potted plants to chamber pots – except the fresh meats, fish, fruits, and vegetables that are sold in the huge and honeycombed central market starting at 6:00 or earlier each morning. There are gold shops and fabric shops and cooking-ware shops and electrical shops and bicycle shops and Honda repair shops and tile shops and rug shops and calligraphy shops and funeral wreath shops and tailor shops and every other kind of shop within the imagination of humankind. All are cheek-by-jowl, all filled with family-employees, customers or passers-by. The effect is hectic and exhilarating – excluding the somnambulant two-hour siesta at lunchtime when everything grinds to a halt and the hammocks are strung and clerks snooze on mats or atop counters in the shops.

We must be nearing the destination; Mota's lips are moving as he squints at numbers. Or perhaps he is praying. It is useless for me to ask as he is a Cambodian and famous in our Motor Pool for speaking Pidgin everything – including, we are assured, even his native tongue. I know that I have personally tried him in French, Vietnamese and English and have found him unresponsive in all. We have now found the magic No. 79, but we are hunting for 79A so it comes as no surprise that this is not the doctor's office. (One would assume that A, B, C, and D of the same number might be reasonably close together. Not so.) Another grumpy and sweaty ten minutes later, we find the A section of the number and our relief is palpable. Mota and I share a friendly cigarette. We have successfully crossed the Rubicon together and now it remains only to find our way home again.

The doctor's sign announces his office hours in both Vietnamese and Chinese. These are mainly the lunch and evening hours and Sunday mornings as the doctor serves in the Vietnamese Army; he must work all of his free time to make a living, as neither the military nor the civil service in Vietnam pay a living wage. I am on his side already.

The doctor's office is not exactly reassuring. The "waiting room" (the larger of the two rooms) is about eight by eight feet square, directly on the street and unfettered by windows or a door. Some cabinets and a bench line each wall; these would certainly provide sufficient space if the whole center of the room were not occupied by two 'luxury' motorbikes. I lean my back against the cool mortar wall, my knees almost touching a Honda.

I know I will remember this room for the rest of my life. I scan it, starting with the spaghetti of wires and a fuse box by the street entrance; from it, wires snake in a dizzying array across ceiling and walls. No problem locating the wiring here if there is an electrical malfunction – if you can just find the right wire. To the right is a faded and all but indistinguishable picture of a lady (I think) in a sedan chair. She adds a certain tone to the place that might otherwise be strictly utilitarian.

The fuse box and the picture completely fill up the wall just opposite me. At right angles is a wall of frosted glass, which gives a hint of privacy to the doctor's inner sanctum. I can just make out a figure bending over the patient and hear the murmur of the doctor's voice through the swinging door from which his nurse (one supposes) emerges periodically to give me a broad smile. She is wearing purple slacks and a print blouse, not the traditional and flattering Vietnamese *ao dai*, indicating that she, too, is probably Chinese.

Against the glass partition leans a bookcase, the contents of which I will list in their entirety: a Wesson oil bottle partially filled with water and beside it a soiled paper cup. An ashtray of brown plastic, badly scarred and containing a tiny cigarette butt. A battered pot with no lid or handle. A feather duster. Not a single book. All these diverse but simple items look surrealistic against the worn book case. On the bench beside me lies a stack of forms printed in Vietnamese and Chinese, stamped in a red caduceus and with the good doctor's name.

I glance down at the floor. It is stained with crankcase oil and a faint splattering of beetle nut juice looking like fresh blood.

My turn finally comes and I am summoned inside by the girl in the purple pants. I never find out who she is as she leaves immediately thereafter and I never see her again. The doctor wears a white coat over his uniform and has one of those ancient 'Dr. Kildare' devices – the round mirror with a hole in the middle – perched at a rakish angle above one eye. He greets me with smiles and a soft voice and peers at me intently as if trying to discern visually the nature of my illness. I then recite my symptoms (the infamous Asian "jungle rot" in the ear). He reacts empathically as he clucks at my discomfort and beams at my intermittent attempts to remedy it. And now he must examine the object of all this misery: the interior of the ears.

I am asked to lie down on a sagging army cot covered with an almost white sheet and a Chinese newspaper at the foot for my feet to rest on. The doctor turns on a 150-watt lightbulb hanging exposed on a cord just over my head. Luckily it is early evening or the heat would be stifling as there is neither window nor fan in this interior room. A gigantic mosquito lights on me and when I surreptitiously crush it on the sheet it makes a large red stain. The doctor examines the offending ears and starts working away like a mad scientist over a liquid on a hotplate on a table nearby, where instruments are also boiling. There's no running water on the premises (rather a handicap for a doctor's office one would think – but then I have seen beauty shops here that also operate without it).

The doctor washes his hands in alcohol and shakes them dry. He mixes chemicals from little vials and ancient-looking murky bottles with glass stoppers. The twentieth century seems far, far away. But I have great faith in this kindly man: I was assured that he is a graduate in otolaryngology from an American university, certainly indicated by his good English. And he's the best on hand right now in Saigon.

He pours ear-droppers full of a murky liquid in my ears and it hurts – and probably hisses and bubbles. (I cast my eyes sideways to see if steam is coming out of them.) He then takes a narrow stick, winds gauze around it and probes and pokes away, removing bits of debris, humming happily as he works. His touch is butterfly light and he winces as I wince, sighs when I sigh. I am totally relaxed in the hands of this benevolent little god.

The willing suspension of disbelief which engulfed me when I walked in does not even leave me when I see him draw at least a shot glass full of some drug into a gigantic hypodermic needle. I do inquire as to what it is and am told it is a mixture of some new drug whose name I do not know. This obviously must go into my ample buttocks as such a quantity could never be introduced into a skinny arm. I hike up my skirt and bare a sun-browned hip. I estimate that I must now have about 10-12 ounces of drugs entering my bloodstream. I idly speculate on the possibility of an acute drug reaction and realize that if this happens, I am dead; who would ever be able to find me here in a remote back street in a big city? Oh well, there is only once to die – unlike jungle rot, which is with us always.

We now have our consultation. I sit by his battered desk while he composes English prose for my consult form. He spells out my disease and the prognosis (not too good as long as I stay in the tropics and continue to swim in local pools) and writes down a list of drugs to take and salves to smear. I am to come back in five days and he will reevaluate. I feel like perhaps we are shooting butterflies with cannons. I now have been in his office for over half an hour but when he rather apologetically states his fee, it is a modest three thousand Piaster (or less than five dollars American), and that includes even the massive shot. I pay him and warmly thank him. I feel like I am parting from an old friend.

Near the car, Mota is hunkered down and smoking. He leaps to his feet and throws open the car door for me then leaps in, starting the car in a flurry of activity and we shoot off in a symphony of un-meshed gears, scattering children, dogs and passing pedestrians before us. Mota wants to get home for dinner – or maybe a hot date? I glance over at his simian features and spiky black hair and wonder what sort of a girl Mota goes for. To me, he is funny and even lovable, but I wonder how a Vietnamese girl might regard that snaggle-tooth smile and the darker cast of the Cambodian skin.

As we drive home, I engage in my favorite pastime: second storey watching. That's where the real fascination lies – after all, shops all look pretty much alike in Southeast Asia. But on balconies, forests spring up: palms and bamboo and great arches of bougainvillea and forsythia. There's the family laundry jutting out over the street on bamboo poles, the grandmother of the family cooling herself in the last rays of sunshine, the pretty young girl leaning out of the window talking to her boyfriend below, the old man burning joss sticks at the family altar, the pigeons in their coops, the cages after cages of banana birds and doves and parakeets and the sparrows fluttering around them trying to cadge grain. It is unendingly fascinating and I mentally plan a possible picture book, perhaps called "Second Storey Saigon".

Mota returns me to my own second storey apartment where I greet my dogs and tend my own turtle doves, water my palm and rubber trees and twine my bougainvillea around its trellis.

3

BIEN HOA AND JOHN PAUL VANN

A FEW WEEKS later in Bien Hoa, I settled into yet another new home, this one was a real apartment, light years better than the Oscar. It was in a utilitarian complex on the outskirts of the small village of Bien Hoa and it housed USAID and other government types stationed in the area. The apartment compound was called the Franzblau, named after a young CORDS civilian advisor and Vann protégé who had died earlier in Vietnam. Best of all, the large apartment building had a roof-top terrace overlooking the airfield, handy for both sunbathing and plane (later rocket) spotting.

Luckily one of the secretaries in my old office had a friend in another agency who had just transferred to Bien Hoa the previous month and shortly after we got there, we both got invited to the mammoth New Year's Eve party that was going to be held on the roof of the Franzblau. I welcomed the opportunity to make some new contacts and to get the lie of the land, so I accepted with alacrity. The evening of December 31, 1967 was a beautiful one. A cool breeze blew across the rooftop, where tables had been set out and a small dance floor laid down to give it a nightclub atmosphere. Food, drink and attentive males – at the usual favorable ratio – were plentiful and the midnight hour approached much too soon.

At that witching hour, if I cannot be with a person I love then I prefer to be alone, so I detached myself from the crowd about three minutes before midnight and went to a darkened corner of the rooftop facing the air base about a hundred yards across a back road. Midnight was prophetic of things to come – only, of course, I could not know that then. Sirens sounded and every American soldier in Vietnam must have shot off a few of rounds of ammo; the sky was laced with tracer bullets and bits of flame spurted up here and there from mortar rounds being fired. The village of Bien Hoa itself was comparatively quiet, this not being a holiday in the Vietnamese culture. Theirs would come several weeks later.

I made a few quick resolutions and then returned to the festivities. There were champagne breakfasts the next day (no big deal; at that time champagne sold in the PX's Class VI store at $2.00 a bottle) followed by the offer of a tour of the air base. This suited me fine as I could use the trip as an excuse to case the layout and the Officers' Club and the swimming pool, around which my life would probably revolve in future months. Both proved to be up to my modest standards. The proximity of my housing to the airfield was all I really cared about and it was nearly at the perimeter fence, although the main (and only) gate was farther up the village's main road. From the rooftop (and later from my bedroom) I could watch choppers and big planes take off and land. When the latter took off from the main runway, their flight path brought them about fifty yards over our roof with a roar that rattled the dishes. Later, I was able to sleep through the noise at 6:00 every morning and not even hear it.

I liked Bien Hoa and everything about it: the air was less smog-filled, the location was ideal for travel into the surrounding countryside and the housing was far better in this recently-completed apartment block. People were also friendlier and more relaxed than their Saigon counterparts, or so it seemed to me. My life was definitely taking a turn for the better.

I could use my VW bug for the commute to my office, into Saigon, and to the various Army facilities including the sprawling Long Binh army base nearby; it had a PX, cinema, pizza parlor – and even a brothel, it was rumored – and, of course, to the air base's clubs and pool that lay so conveniently close. This was the home base of the (later infamous) defoliators, called the "Ranch Hands". These were the pilots who flew low-level missions over suspected Viet Cong hide-outs, dropping toxic "Agent Orange" (named for its color) to kill all the trees and jungle cover that hid them. It also killed field crops and, as we were to find out much later, people. The Ranch Hands had created their own esprit, logo, and even an off-duty uniform: a flight suit in bright purple, always topped by a white silk scarf wrapped around the neck.

As I drove through the streets of Bien Hoa on my first day there, I marveled that any place could be so unlovely. The town had once been no more than a village and now was filled with an ever-growing population due primarily to the war and the air base that formed its northern boundary. The air base had been originally built by the French, then taken over by the Japanese, then again by the French, then by the Vietnamese and finally, within the last ten years, shared by the Americans. The American section, separated from the Vietnamese portion by barbed wire and guards at the entrance, was typically military: all khaki and concrete and sandbags.

The Vietnamese portion was composed of gently decaying white two-storey stucco buildings in the French colonial style, their windows framed by louvered shutters and their roofs of dark tiles, all slightly shabby but still far more attractive than the American cantonment. In France's heyday, this base must have been a select military assignment. Now it was sprawling, overcrowded and ugly – and now reputedly the busiest airport in the world with a recorded 857,000 take-offs and landings per year. This did include, however, all chopper take-offs and landings, handled on a separate section of the base – over by our quarters, as a matter of fact – some distance from the two main runways. But the description was still apt. With the exception of the monsoon season, the whole time I lived in Bien Hoa, I think I almost never looked up at the sky when there was not an airplane of some description visible or audible. You can well imagine what the noise level was like, especially at 6:00 in the morning and 5:00 in the evening when the choppers returned from ferrying troops out to war. Vann once claimed to newspapermen that ninety-five percent of the U.S. troops in III Corps slept between white sheets every night. When challenged by the Embassy hierarchy in Saigon to prove this within twenty-fours or retract it, he did – to their ire and chagrin.

The village of Bien Hoa, with the Dong Nai River flowing through its outskirts, was a strewn accumulation one-story stucco shops with latticed metal shutters that were pulled down at night. Glass was rare in these buildings; this was fortunate in that it reduced the danger of flying glass in the later attacks. There were no large general stores, only the usual street-side shops that carried a range of merchandise, now including items which might appeal to the newly-arrived GIs (some of it having been "liberated" from American supplies). Each local store had its own specialty: bread and cakes, locally-made ceramics, tailoring, motorbike and bicycle parts, daily-use items, etc.

Prominent in the scheme were the new bars with their appealing but totally incongruous American names like the Miami, the Copacabana, the Ritz, or sometimes something simpler and accurate like Rosie's Place. These were all the same old stucco buildings but with elaborately-painted wooden doors behind their metal grills. A bar lined one wall and the remaining space was taken up by tiny tables and stools; a bandstand of sorts usually occupied the space at the rear although blaring, canned music often supplied the sound, except on Saturday nights. The bars were always dark, enhancing the beauty of the Vietnamese bar girls and making the mishandling of money even easier. Prices started at about $2.00 for the glass of "Saigon tea" that you were obliged to buy for a girl to obtain even her momentary attention. A mixed drink of black market American whiskey sold for $2.00 upward and beer ran about fifty cents a glass. Even at those low prices, few GIs ever emerged from the bars with much money left in their pockets. Prostitution of course flourished in the network of small buildings that radiated from the alleys that lay back of the bars.

The streets of Bien Hoa were mostly paved, but rutted and pot-holed by the heavy trucks that moved over them in a steady stream. There were few sidewalks and the street vendors' wares sometimes spilled out onto the streets; this combined with the heavy pedestrian and pedicab traffic to make comfortable movement virtually impossible. Vehicles crawled alongside and around pedestrians and the occasional oxcart. At night, drunk GIs careened back and forth between bars (that composed about fifty percent of all the structures during those days) as hookers grabbed at the arms of the ambulant GIs ones who still remained unescorted. There was much shouting and joviality and the whole effect was like a small and dirty Rio in carnival time, sprawling, brawling – and a good time was had by all.

Young Vietnamese kids moved in and out of the throng selling everything from warm Coca-Colas to Japanese prophylactics, with a little pickpocketing on the side. Occasional screaming fights between prostitutes and their patrons, bar-owners and their clientele, or sometimes GI vs. GI livened up the nights and drew interested onlookers. I was glad that I had seen what a typical Vietnamese "wartime" village was like. A few weeks later it would be radically changed, and never returned to normal again during the remainder of my stay there.

I was glad I had bought a Volkswagen while in Saigon as it offered more freedom of movement and quicker access to the office from the Franzblau Apartments. The apartment complex was devoid of charm but was a luxury building by the local standards: two concrete apartment blocks containing one- and two-bedroom units and, although relatively modest, at three storeys, it was one of the taller buildings in Bien Hoa. The courtyard, devoid of grass and trees, was used as a secure parking lot. A high concrete wall topped with concertina wire surrounded the compound and a series of Vietnamese guards manned the only gate. Behind the compound were the squatters' shacks that lined the airfield's perimeter fence, some of them actually leaning against our compound walls.

I was assigned an apartment on the ground floor on the side nearest the airfield. It consisted of a living room, a bedroom with bath on the back of the building and a small kitchen to the side of the main door fronting on the main hallway that ran down the center of the building. The only window in the kitchen gave out onto this hallway, thus sharing its cooking smells with the entire building. Later, in nights of mortar and rocket attacks, this small, windowless and sheltered room became a very popular location.

The apartment was fully furnished and I was delighted to see that some generous buyer had chosen really nice Hong Kong-made teak furniture. The upholstered chairs and sofa were Danish Modern and the tables and beds were stained teakwood. French windows opened out onto the dreary back lot still partially filled with detritus from the building process. The guard force of maybe ten Vietnamese lived year-round in makeshift quarters against the back walls or in summer on cots that they placed under the overhang of the balconies above us.

They apparently sent out for most of their food, the take-out trade being a universal one in Vietnam, but they did brew their tea over a Sterno flame, washed their clothes at the water faucet in the back and attended to their other needs at a toilet and washroom nestled in the corner of the back lot. I felt I was living with them when the windows were open, their high, sing-songy voices drifting in as they often walked past my window, staring in with interest. I had the lucky distinction of being one of five women then living in the building but the only one living on the ground floor. The only inconvenience was that I had to remain fully dressed as long as the drapes were open – but this relaxed a bit when I discovered they were not in the slightest interested in my anatomy, only in my lifestyle.

Outside the front door of our building was a large brass plaque setting forth the particulars of the death of Robert Franzblau for whom the complex was named. He had been a 24-year-old USAID employee who had served in Vietnam for four years, first with the Army as a Lieutenant and then with CORDS, our aid organization in the provinces. Vann had personally picked him and assigned him to the province where he was killed only a few months after taking on the job. He had been visiting the district chief and his wife and then had decided to spend the night in the village even though VC were known to be in the area. That night, the VC chose to assassinate the chief and his wife, and since Robert was there it was necessary to kill him too.

He was beloved by the Vietnamese and he had even planned to marry a Saigon girl. I later found out that he was the only son of wealthy parents, a "golden boy" of great intellect and promise who was vitally interested in helping the Vietnamese. He was also one of the best of the bright young men we had in CORDS.

I found the old truism to be valid in the months that followed: often the brightest and best were the first ones felled, while the lesser lights emerged unscathed.

From the Franzblau apartments you turned right outside the main gate to get to the CORDS Headquarters, currently housed in the old "Autumn Cloud" whorehouse. I was told that eager clients still tried to get into the building, remembering it from happier days. The CORDS compound was surrounded by concrete walls with an alleyway just beyond it that led to a cluster of houses behind the back wall where many Vietnamese families lived.

We always had cheerful Vietnamese children playing around the guards and drivers in that back lane – I hardly ever saw a child cry except in most dire circumstances. We had our favorites, including one spunky, bright-eyed boy of about three whose mother was a prostitute and whose father she claimed was an Air Force major (although we suspected a notoriously randy MP of a previous tour). The mother and her friends were still practicing their trade there behind our back walls; this made the alley a busy thoroughfare, with her home a choice location from the standpoint of convenience to potential clients. Joe, as we called him, was an enchanting child, loving and happy, and at any given time there was always someone who was talking of trying to adopt him and take him back to the US; someday it may happen, but would he be any happier there? Vietnamese children do not wear diapers and run around like playful puppies. After seeing children without diapers for so long, you realize how really deformed our American children look with bulky diapers giving their small bodies a bottom-heavy look and making their walking awkward. Little brown bare bottoms are infinitely more appealing despite the somewhat unlovely consequences.

The trip from the Franzblau to CORDS had become more difficult because one of the few well-paved streets had been in a continual process of being ripped up to facilitate the laying of a new sewage line, a thoughtful gift from the Australians that we cursed daily as traffic snarled and our cars plowed over gullies bridged by PSP (Pierced Steel Planking, used all over wartime Vietnam). The construction had already been in process for over a year when I got to Bien Hoa, and it was not yet completed a year later when I left; we simply learned to regard the open trenches as a permanent part of the landscape, providing welcomed work for a number of Vietnamese who often leaned on their shovels to watch the passing parade of foreigners.

On our left we passed a half-finished school, an AID project which had also been bogged down due to a problem with funding (much of probably siphoned off locally). It stood as a permanent reminder to the population, I suppose, that we promised much and sometimes delivered somewhat less. About halfway up the street, past the main gate of the airfield, we came to a traffic circle on which there was a gas station and a police station; the CORDS headquarters lay a half block off this circle. Its proximity to the police station should have been a comfort, but in view of the fact that the police were spasmodically a target for attacks, sometimes with mortars, often badly aimed, we regarded it with somewhat less than enthusiasm.

With the exception of the small cluster of houses back of the headquarters compound, the area was often flooded. Paddy fields stretched along both sides of Quoc 191 (Route Nationale 1, formerly a main artery leading north from Saigon to Hanoi) toward the bridges spanning the Dong Nai River about a mile away. There was a Military Police station up the road where Vann's chopper had a landing pad and the "Aussie Hotel," that housed an Australian medical team and Vann's pilot, an Army captain of volatile disposition and daring flying skills (which

Vann admired as his were equally daring). When you first flew toward the CORDS pad by chopper you had the feeling you were going to land in water since the MP's small concrete landing complex covered the only high ground in the area.

I soon settled into the "Head Shed" office routine, one that was a refreshing change from the USAID squirrel cage in Saigon. It was a busy place with the comings and goings of the American staff, officers, civilians and Vietnamese officials and their hangers-on, plus the supplicants whom Vann seemed to attract. He had the power and the chutzpah to cut corners and get things done and a lot of people wanted to tap into that. But first they had to get past his secretary, Frenchy. She was not French but a tough Jewish gal from the Bronx who was able to match Vann in profanity. She served as his stalwart gate guardian. If you were able to smooth-talk your way past Frenchy, no mean feat, you just might get in to see Vann.

Frenchy had her favorites – I called them "The Anointed" – but if you were not one then fat chance. I remember one poor major trying to see Vann for days but he apparently had not been suitably deferential to Frenchy. He had learned his lesson, however, and from my office next door I heard him, now humbled, plead that he had tried to see Vann at least five times but still had not gotten in to see him. Frenchy, still in her "take no prisoners" mode, gave him her famous fish-eye stare and delivered the death knell: "And you never will." And I doubt he ever did.

In our office, I worked for the No. 2 man and also backed up Frenchy. She was generally pleasant to me but I was careful never to cross her – I just tried to keep out of her way. But she was a dynamo and I soon also learned how to juggle ten tasks at once: sorting out visitors – although I lacked Frenchy's famed firewall ability – typing reports, answering phones and deciding which messages were critical and which were merely important, running errands to pick up papers and stuff for Vann to carry on his frequent visits to the field, and in general being a dogsbody. We worked long hours and we worked hard but being in the field was way better than at a desk-bound job in Saigon.

My favorite part of the job was making and taking calls on the hand-cranked field phone. Then I could shout things that I had only heard in World War II movies, use words like "over" and "out" to alternate and end messages, all that sort of stuff. I had already learned my ABCs – the Able-Baker-Charlies – and I took to that phone like a duck to water. Which was fortunate as I later was able to use my expertise down in Can Tho.

Vann's title was technically Director of III Corps in USAID parlance but was shortened to Deputy for CORDS or DEPCORDS. His No. 2, an old comrade-in-arms, was thus the A/DEPCORDS. In my new job I would be the Number 2 secretary and work first for Colonel Wilbur Wilson and as back-up for Vann, a double treat (or as we sometimes called it, a "double whammy").

Our offices were adjoining at the front of the main building with the larger office for Vann and the smaller for Frenchy. Both were duplicated on my side of a center aisle with Colonel Wilson and my offices. All faced the road but there was no way of seeing it since on the first floor all the windows were of glass brick for security reasons. Back of these offices were those of the Executive Secretary, a Light (or Lieutenant) Colonel, and of Vann's aide, a young Lieutenant, plus the Military Senior Adviser, a Bird (or full) Colonel, and other military types.

My office was nearest the door of our side of the complex and one of my many jobs was to screen visitors who came in our door, supposedly a separate entrance just for Vann and his staff but used by everyone from people looking for the MP station to lost GIs. With the number of people in and out of the offices all day, my office was about as conducive to concentrated work as the men's room of the YMCA – in fact, when I saw the skewed ratio of men to women, I often felt I was working in a YMCA.

My boss turned out to be even more famous in the military than Vann (who had also been an Army Colonel). He was both feared and revered and better known by the nickname "Coalbin Willie". He was a legend in the US Army and had gotten his nickname from the time he was training troops at Ft. Bragg. The stories vary but there were two that I heard more often: One that he had once been the most senior Colonel in the Army and as such felt that the base was not "strac" (tidy) enough. To remedy this, among other things, he ordered that in the bins behind the barracks the coal must be stacked and maintained so that it sloped uniformly from the high to the low end of the bins.

The second, and I think less plausible story, was that for an upcoming inspection he ordered the coal bins to be whitewashed and – or so it was reported – also the coal itself. I liked that story best, and as I got to know him better, I could believe both stories. And also the one explaining his bachelorhood: "If the Army had wanted me to have a wife it would have issued me one." He did not have much use for women in general, but when he found that I did not chatter or "gad about" we got along fine.

He was a solid, erect and taciturn old soldier, then over sixty but looking ten years younger despite his shock of white hair. He spoke only when he had something to say – in the office, of course, it was always related to the job at hand. He had very emphatic ideas about everything and ran a tight ship; he could not tolerate stupidity, sloth or excuses and he did not go easy on the offenders. He bellowed at the cowed victim, his profanity topped only by Vann's own – and that topped by Frenchy, whose colorful vocabulary would have made a sailor blush.

Frenchy was tough as nails, but she was a great worker, fast, highly organized and intuitive (especially as divining what Vann wanted or would need). And I am sure the perfect secretary for him. She had her enemies, those she had shut out from Vann, or insulted or cursed. A fellow officer once asked Vann how he could tolerate her and he had replied that she got things done – meaning done just the way Vann wanted them done, so I think she took the heat (not that she cared a whit) for stuff he did not want to or people he did not want to see. She indeed must have been very useful to him or she would long ago have been gone.

Being a non-confronter (read wimp), I was cordial but not particularly chummy with her, which was really not important or even noticeable in a busy office where we all worked flat out, she for Vann, I for Colonel Wilson plus for whomever handed me something to be done. The "mission" was the ultimate goal, so just get it done! But one day I must have somehow crossed Frenchy, or encroached on her fiefdom, and she told me to go f**k myself. I was stunned, as I had never heard that word spoken by a woman. (A Southern Girl's mantra was: "We don't cuss / And we don't chew / And we don't go / With boys who do.")

As I had no reply (and would have been too intimidated to "talk back" anyway), I just turned and went about my own business on the other side of the aisle. After about an hour she asked me some (inconsequential) question and I answered Yes, or No, nothing else. A little later she tried again and got another monosyllable from me. As the day progressed, she got more and more friendly, then asked if I also wanted to order a cup of coffee, such little overtures of increasing friendliness. By the end of the day, she spent more time trying to be nice to me than I had seen in the previous month. I held out to the very end and the next day it was business as usual for both of us. But she never again cursed me.

The bosses initially made concessions to the fact that I was a Southern Lady. Colonel Wilson was most amusing when talking

33

to Vann or another staff member: he would lower his voice on the crucial word so I could not hear it in the outer office. Thus the conversation would go: "…and I told that goddamn mother (mumble) that if he did not get off his (mumble-mumble) and get his (mumble) in gear I was going to kick him in the (mumble). He's so Goddamn (mumble) scared that he (mumbles) in his pants every time the (mumble) artillery fires." But gradually they decided I could take it and the mumbles were replaced by the real article; their conversations then became much less fill-in-the-blank ones.

I tried to anticipate his wishes and did them without a word. If I erred I apologized with a "sorry", offering neither explanation nor excuse – and then I did it right the next time. When I would, early on, inquire if something had been done right, he would tell me not to worry, I'd know soon enough if it wasn't. He would sometimes offer us all a few words of advice such as, "Goddamit don't think for yourself, just do what I say!" or "There you go thinking again, weakening the team." (It's a handy phrase which I still use). Or when some big planning session produced nothing of value as far as he could see: "The elephants after heavy labor have given birth to a mouse." My favorite, however, was the observation that the presence of us American women in Vietnam was "like being a virgin on a troop train'. Who could say it better?

Colonel Wilson was compulsively neat, so I made sure that all papers were labeled and stacked neatly in his In-Box. At first he carried out office business with little concession to my existence; in fact I don't think he even saw me most of the time. There was no malice in it; he just did not believe women should be in the combat zone and hence I suppose for him I simply was not there. But after a month or so, he addressed his first direct social comment to me: a haruummppp and a "Morning." As he had previously entered and exited with scarcely a glance, this unexpected cordiality stunned me, but from then onward I was treated as "one of the boys".

By then, I had seen Colonel Wilson in action and had the greatest respect and admiration for him; he was smart, salty and solid as a rock. I believe I really got his attention, however, when I showed interest in the stock market. He then started giving me stock market tips. (I would have done well to follow them, as he was rumored to have been the richest colonel in the Army.)

I also think Colonel Wilson, like Vann, was totally without fear. It wasn't that they were brave – which connotes the over-coming of fear – it was simply not part of their makeup (Wilson's bravery was amply documented when he fought with the 82nd Airborne in the invasion of Normandy and onward). He was fearless and God help those who were not – they got short shrift from him. Colonel Wilson and Mr. Vann – we always addressed them that way – were clearly cut from the same cloth and they worked well together. They had both retired from the Army and shared many similar characteristics: neither suffered fools gladly, both had short fuses, and both were constantly and colorfully profane. You could not have asked for two better bosses – or a more exciting place to work. And it was soon to become even more exciting.

One of the more pleasant aspects of my job was greeting the visitors who swarmed like locusts at our headquarters. That meant that I got to meet both powerful and also colorful and in-teresting men, like the VIPs and war correspondents who wanted to meet and talk to (often at time-consuming length) the famous – or infamous – John Paul Vann. He was a favorite source of in-formation for correspondents; he was always good for a pithy or colorful quote.

He and Colonel Wilson had little respect for many of these

Washington VIPs who were often strap-hangers with little knowl-
edge and even less interest in Vietnam itself; they were there to
show the voters and colleagues how gutsy they were – and to
experience some of the exotica of the 'Orient' at the taxpayers'
expense. Few had taken the trouble to do their homework and
I was often surprised that they had done so little and knew so
little. They had no idea of protocol and tended to want to wear
lurid Hawaiian sports shirts when meeting Vietnamese officials,
these French-trained Vietnamese comprising the country's elite
and ruling class.

In Vietnam, the top political figures were not simple provin-
cials and they were keenly aware of the subtleties of protocol. I
once heard Vann giving some succinct instructions, at the top
of his lungs, to the protocol officer in Saigon; all telephone conversations with Saigon (and almost everywhere else) were carried on at full volume due to the dodgy connections at all times:
"Goddammit, they get dressed up when they go out to screw the
Vietnamese women so they can damn well get dressed to meet
the province chief. These people are not fools, which is more than
I can say of Senator X. They know what's going on! I'll not have
any VIP in my province who can't dress for a protocol affair, so
don't bother to send them down here unless you've told them
that, or you dress 'em yourself! Is that clear?"

It apparently was, as the conversation ended abruptly.

In retrospect, I cannot recall ever seeing Vann in anything but
a white sports shirt and khaki pants, his standard work uniform
except for awards and other ceremonies when he wore a narrow
black knit tie, perhaps the only one he owned.

Just outside Vann's office was the two-way radio that connected us with the Province Senior Advisor – the senior USAID
rep – in each of the twelve province capitals. The main set was
monitored upstairs but when the message was for Vann person-

ally, or when he wanted to send one, it was done from his office. When he was not in his office, we often kept the lines open so we could hear what was going on in the provinces. Within our small office complex, in addition to that radio set and the two field phones connected with the Hurricane switchboard there were several other outside lines, all of which we had to monitor and answer. As there were only two doors to the office complex, the front one for us and the side one for visitors, there was always someone coming or going. That plus the constant attendance to the phones kept us all hopping around like trained fleas.

The work day started at 8:00am and ended at 6:00pm with a two-hour lunch break – if we could get it. There was no place to go for lunch except home or to the O Club at the air base, unless you wanted to eat upstairs in the Vietnamese-run snack bar on the roof of our building. Its standards were a little less than ideal which made eating there a sort of Russian Roulette as you didn't know what you might get, either in terms of food or diseases. We discovered that a scrambled egg sandwich was the safest bet as there's not too much you can do to screw up an egg. And if you could not make yourself understood verbally you could always make cackling noises and flap your arms like a chicken – to the great amusement of onlookers.

I rapidly settled into my new life. I had thought I would be driving back to Saigon frequently to visit friends and take advantage of its limited cultural offerings, which were still 100% more than Bien Hoa's, but as soon as I got out of Saigon I discovered that I had no desire whatsoever to go back. In fact, I would not even have gone at all if I had not chosen to make the bi-weekly run to the commissary. We had fully-equipped kitchens and our servants could buy bread, fish and fresh vegetables in the local market, but meats and staples plus American-brand foodstuffs had to come from the military in Saigon's commissary. Traffic on the Bien Hoa-Saigon stretch of highway even on the best of days was awful; the dirt, heat and noise combined with the heavy traffic into Cholon, the section of Saigon that housed the PX and Commissary (more on which later), made the trip a formidable undertaking usually consuming a half day and fraying one's nerves – but it had to be done if you wanted to eat "American style" at home.

In addition to the Bien Hoa air base's O Club (Officers' Club), there was the Officers' Open Mess at the nearby Train Compound, the Army base which housed the military advisors to the Vietnamese. Both were open to us civilians but when I got home dead tired at 6:30 or 7:00 at night I had little desire to get redressed to go out to eat, especially as I made a point of trying to look my best whenever I went to dine in any military facility.

There were so few American women in Bien Hoa that I felt the least I could do was to dress brightly and femininely and slosh on lots of perfume; there was just too much green and khaki around and I felt the troops deserved better from an American female. A more appreciative audience you could not have found; even the simplest dress – and by then they were already getting pretty short – brought comments and often whistles of appreciation. I, then a summer blonde but one who would win no beauty prizes anywhere in the world, was asked more than once when wearing an especially crowd-pleasing outfit (one that would go unnoticed in the US) if I were an entertainer of some kind.

It was a standing joke that we Round Eyes in Vietnam were part of Lady Bird Johnson's Beautification Campaign: send all ugly girls to Vietnam. We always had to try to live this down, not easy in a climate where the makeup often sweated right off your face and long hair either frizzed or went limp in two minutes in the tropical heat. But then with a ratio of ten-thousand-plus to one, there was not too much an American female could do wrong.

Right across the hall from me in the building lived Lucy, a very popular former Air Force nurse who stood nearly six feet tall and weighed in at about 180 pounds. She had bright red hair and an equally colorful vocabulary, plus an awesome liquor capacity that would put a stevedore to shame. I had gotten to know her when late one night she had staggered to my door, glassy-eyed and knee-walking drunk, thinking it was her apartment. I gently steered her across the corridor and saw her safely in where she then collapsed onto her sofa; I am sure she spent the night there.

I had had many invites to dinner from the men in the apartment complex but since they were all married, and since I felt that too much apartment co-mingling was practically incestuous, I had turned them all down. Probably also because I was still hoping to re-establish a relationship I had developed with Dave, my "Saigon Warrior", a funny, tall and handsome CIA guy I had gotten quite attached to in my short stay there. I was rather upset that he had not shown up, as promised, on my first weekend in Bien Hoa. But when dates are broken in Vietnam, it could be for many reasons: lack of transportation, subsequent assignment or just a general SNAFU, so we never got really upset about it. I did wonder, however, what had happened and why I had not heard from him. Anyway, I had also decided the least I could do was to refrain from "runnin' around" the minute I hit Bien Hoa, even if I was so inclined – which I was not (well, at least at that time).

After about a week of my own cooking – how many peanut butter sandwiches can one eat anyway? – and before I had found an amah (servant) who was a good cook I asked Lucy if she would like to dress up and accompany me to the O Club. I would not ordinarily do this on a weekend but I felt that going there mid-week was a little less conspicuous, especially if we went early and did not hang around in the bar. I hated the whole idea of looking like I was waiting to be picked up (consequently I have never gone into a bar alone in my life). I was not going to make an exception to that rule, even though I knew it might work a hardship on Lucy, who had a reputation for being a bit of a lush.

When I went across the hall to pick her up, I was hardly prepared for the sight: she wore a close-fitting yellow number that would have been a bit less striking if she had not overflowed it at the top and strained all the seams. As I had chosen that night to wear a bright orange dress, no one could possibly miss us on this occasion – we practically glowed in the dark. When we walked into the O Club and every eye became riveted on us, I became increasingly shy – an emotion which ordinarily does not plague me – when I realized we must have looked like two broads gussied up like birds of paradise.

I suppressed an impulse to flee and managed to persuade Lucy that we should go to the restaurant at once and not into the bar – no mean feat, I might add. All I wanted was to sit down away from so many staring eyeballs as soon as possible. In the main diningroom we started looking around for a place to sit. All the tables were for four to eight and all were partially filled. As we stared into a sea of faces, two tall men stood up and waved us over to their table. I looked at Lucy and when I saw her friendly smile I figured they were her friends. We were relieved to find a seat and joined them at their table. After a few minutes of conversation, it was clear that Lucy had never met them before, but by then we were chatting away with the relief of having found a pleasant haven.

Our hosts introduced themselves to us as Big Bob and Don – Don being even bigger than Big Bob – both pilots with the 12th Air Command Squadron of the Ranch Hands. They told us that their job was to defoliate thick jungle growth by spraying toxic pesticides from a height of 50 feet above treetop at 120 knots airspeed – not easy with lumbering C-130s that try to fall out of the sky at that speed. They assured us that it was one of the most dangerous jobs in Vietnam. That they were pilots spoke for itself, not only in their dress but in their brashness and chutzpah. In my subsequent tours in Vietnam, whenever I saw men move in rapidly to snake women aside for themselves, they almost inevitably turned out to be pilots. I never knew whether they were living up to their reputation or just busy earning it.

Big Bob had me monopolized within a matter of minutes and was trying all the standard moves. He soon realized I wasn't buying any of it but that set him back only temporarily. I had a feeling that he previously had not had a notable lack of success with the opposite sex. I told him flatly that it was my policy not to mess around with married men, that he was obviously married and that was that. He parried that by stating that he was "separated". Months later, when I called him out for lying about being married, he replied with great patience as if to a child: "If I'd told you I was married you wouldn't have had anything to do with me, dummy!"

I had to admit the logic of that but I could not help but be dumbfounded at the simplicity with which men can rationalize in that predatory field – and how easily we females fall for it. I had to chide myself for my "willing suspension of disbelief", so I guess in the long run it evened out. (And soon I was to learn that in Vietnam, when a guy said he was "separated' it simply meant separated by the Pacific Ocean.)

During the meal we played the usual "What do you do in Real Life?" game. That life for Bob had been eighteen years in the Air Force and now with the Ranch Hands' special operations squadron. Mine was university teaching and now a Foreign Service career; there was thus little common ground between us – except for Time and Place. He also told me that defoliation was one of the dirtiest and most dangerous jobs in Vietnam; I found that a bit of a stretch and took it for the usual bravado bullflop. He in turn faked fascination at a dubious tale I told of driving through "Charlie country" (meaning through Viet Cong-controlled countryside).

I had indeed done this one weekend and offered to take him along on my next trip – which he declined with alacrity, saying he was no bloody hero and didn't intend to be one. He did agree that he would like to drive out some weekend into the nearby countryside with me. That was tempting, but I told him we should wait until after the upcoming Tet holiday when we might have some mutual days off from my work and his flying.

We finally compromised that he would have me out to dinner at the base, this after seeing that, despite broad hints, I was not about to invite him down to my apartment for dinner. He was a fun guy and his patter quite entertaining, but he was much too fast an operator to really interest me. I had dated pilots before and found their snake-oil charm a bit overwhelming; they felt any time not spent in direct pursuit of sex to be time wasted – and they did not like to waste time.

This settled, I collected a now thoroughly-soused Lucy, we bade a fond farewell to the entire boozy bunch and I drove us back to the Franzblau. Lucy had also been invited for dinner the next night, not by Don but by another of his hooch mates whom she really did seem to know. This made an interesting combination as Jeff weighed about 125 pounds and stood 5'7" so Lucy towered over him. Even though they looked like a Mutt and Jeff together, they still had one major attribute in common: a love for liquor and a tremendous capacity for it. I was pretty sure they were going to be soul mates.

The next night, we first spent a spell in the O Club bar, a low-ceilinged and dimly-lighted hole with air-conditioning at a level just above freezing. You had to drink to keep warm, an interesting twist for the tropics (but maybe just a clever tool to increase bar boozing?). The place was about half-filled with Ranch Hands and the other half with fighter pilots who kept coming by our table and waiting – always in vain – to be introduced. Bob sent them off laughing at his shtick and it was soon obvious that our popularity was as much due to Bob's quick wit as to the fact that he had corralled two of the rare local Round Eyes.

I'm pretty fast on my feet verbally but Bob usually got in the last word – which increased his stature in my eyes; there are not too many men who can top me in the smart-ass department. I could outsmart them, which of course made me lose interest. I looked at Bob with renewed attention; he just might be a man to be reckoned with. But as I still felt loyalty to Dave up in Saigon, so I was not really interested in sleeping with Bob – if for no other reason than that he was obviously used to scoring on the first date. I was simply going to prolong the showdown as long as possible and then write him off after that.

But Bob soon revealed an instinct for handling women – or at least for handling me. Before the end of the evening he had cut off my drinking. (I drink so little that two mixed drinks usually have me higher than a Georgia pine and three put me to sleep.) He also corrected my misconceptions about what I was going to eat for dinner and subtly started controlling my casual flirtation with a cute guy at the next table. Before the evening was over, he was angling for an invite down to my apartment "for a drink."

When I told him that I didn't keep liquor on hand – one of my little lies that cut down considerably on potential freeloaders and parlor snakes – he even volunteered to bring his own. I hedged a little but finally agreed when it turned out that Jeff was going home with Lucy – thus the old "safety in numbers" bit. (I am old enough by now to have learned better, but the one thing I learn from experience is that I don't seem to learn from experience.) By now I felt like reasserting myself and made it clear that I didn't like being a taxi service and that I was bringing both guys back at midnight, regardless, and blah, blah, blah. They accepted this graciously even though I knew I was being a bitch, which made me feel guilty and irritable – thus setting the tone for the rest of the evening.

We exited, amid some ribaldry from the Ranch Hands about our probable purpose in leaving so early, and walked through the compound to my car. The MP on duty saluted briskly, even though Bob and Jeff were in civilian clothes, and then broke into a big grin when Bob greeted him by name as we paused and made small talk with him. We drove through the darkened streets – streetlights being relatively rare in provincial towns – to the Franzblau.

There, the pattern ran predictably when Jeff and Lucy immediately went off to her flat – so much for the old safety in numbers! Bob and I went on down to my place where I fixed him a cup of coffee. I launched into a spiel of bright, pointless chatter which I only resort to when I feel cornered. I waited for Bob to pounce and gradually relaxed when he seemed disinclined to make his move. We gradually got to talking about things which really interested me: airplanes, his job, a lot of Vietnam War stories, our evaluation of rumors regarding the predicted offensive ("not going to happen"), little glimpses into our childhoods and the usual exchanges that evolve when you begin to explore each other's worlds.

I was startled when he announced that it was time to be heading back – I'm usually the timekeeper. I hadn't realized how much time had passed, so engrossed had I been in what we were talking about. As we walked to the door I tried to figure out hastily how to out-maneuver him but it did not prove necessary; he walked out as unconcernedly as if he did not have at his side such a precious commodity as one of the few Round Eyes with sex appeal within fifty square miles. I felt more disgruntled and off-base than ever.

We stopped by to pick up Lucy. A tap at her door brought a slow response and it opened to reveal a truly awe-inspiring sight: Lucy in a sort of chenille jumpsuit which fit like her skin and was bright red; in it, her generous proportions were even larger than they had appeared in a dress, if that were possible. Her eyes were glassy and her speech slurred but she was still vertical, which was more than Jeff was; he was slumped on the sofa, drink still tightly in hand but virtually comatose. He was able to convey, however, that he didn't want to go back to the base that night after all. Bob grinned at me and we hastily bade them farewell. "Good luck," Bob murmured under his breath as we left the happy pair. I could only hope she would not fall on him and crush him to death.

Bob did not like women driving when he was in the car so insisted on driving back to the base himself. It was almost curfew by then – the gates officially closed for the military at midnight – and we got in just under the wire. He explained to the guards that I would be back out in a few minutes; they just smiled knowingly. The O Club was closing down as we went by and Bob honked and waved at his friends as we went past and they cursed us for not picking them up. He then turned in the "No Entry" gate and went up the "Off Limits to Vehicles" street until we parked directly in front of his hooch, which rocked with music and raucous laughter. We were now in an area where a female foot had never trod; men wandered by in their underwear carrying towels on the way to the latrines and showers.

When I declined an invitation to stay for the party, Bob then suggested I come again for dinner the next night and I declined that too; I was still expecting a call from Dave. If he had not come down last weekend then he surely would come this one. Bob's attitude at this point clearly reflected "to hell with you, baby". I knew that unless I tempered the refusals somewhat, this was probably the last I would see of him. I timidly suggested that I might like to come the next Saturday after work and maybe meet his hooch mates and see his quarters if I did not have Saigon visitors (yes, I used the plural). I asked if he would care to call me at the office Saturday morning to confirm. As he had no mission scheduled that morning, he agreed – although I really did not think he'd call. He bade me a casual goodnight and wandered into the hooch without even looking back. This irritated me and I roared off, scattering GIs in my path; I made it back out the main gate just before the barriers went down. Brinksmanship!

When Friday night had brought no word from Dave, I moped around in the flat feeling fretful and sorry for myself. I was by now sure that Bob would not call me the next day either so when he did, my voice must have registered genuine enthusiasm. We had an enjoyable dinner together and then went up to his hooch. I was given the guided tour and introduced to his hooch mates: Mike, an amateur boxer in his college days who teamed up with Bob to prevail in any bar brawls; Norm, a big, cynical and fitting foil for Bob's wit; and Jeff, the smallest of the lot and a big fan of big Lucy.

They were all majors and command pilots and had been together for the last three years, in Commander's Staff College, and had even flown to Vietnam together. They also shared a fondness for broads and booze, of which they could drink prodigious quantities – and which they were in the process of doing when I entered the hooch. They shared a four-man hooch that was nothing more than a tin-roofed wooden structure with screened windows with wooden louvers. These let down when it rained, although they were rather ineffectual in keeping a heavy monsoon rain out, but during the day they were propped open on poles. The hooch was about thirty feet wide and was subdivided into three separate areas: two double bedrooms, with a cot on each side of the rooms' center aisle, plus a living room with a bar in the front half.

The bar not only served as the social center but also as a casual kitchen, with a hotplate and refrigerator completing the ensemble. The walls were decorated with Snoopy drawings – always in flying helmet, of course – and on the door was a huge rendering of the Chinese word for purple, painted in purple, naturally. This was the code name for the defoliant that was used in the raids. The color had morphed into a Ranch Hand symbol and was stenciled in significant places all over the base, including the latrines of the jet jockeys who were the Ranch Hands' chief competition for attention and honors. It was also embroidered on the white silk scarves that Premier Ky had authorized the Ranch Hands to wear with their uniforms. The Ranch Hands did not fly in those scarves, as there was said to be a high price on their heads and the possibility of getting captured in identifying scarves was not too appealing. Without those – and the plane – they looked just like Army guys.

We sat around the bar as the guys told their "covered wagon" tales for my benefit, delighted to have a new and appreciative audience. Liquor flowed like water – actually more plentifully as there was no running water in the hooch. All drinking water came out of the five-gallon plastic jugs on top of the refrigerator, to be refilled from the base's water point. Pilots came and went and were greeted with various degrees of enthusiasm. I asked the usual naive questions:

Q: "Do you-all wear parachutes?"

A: "Are you out of your squash?! We fly fifty feet over the treetops at 120 knots. Where tha hell we supposed to jump to?"

Q: "Are you armed?"

A: "Yep, each with a .45 and usually someone has a carbine along. Oh yes, and maybe a knife strapped to my leg."

I had noted on the bulletin board by the door an interesting "Instructions from the Escape and Evasion Department". It included all the standard items you would expect plus item 10, a little homily which read: "Each man should have a minimum of 500 Piasters to pay for transportation or to scatter behind you to delay your pursuers – they'll get it anyways." There were other little goodies on the bulletin board but none that conjured up such a delightful vision of a redneck happily punching away at his typewriter in a blaze of creativity. Prominent also was a list of rules to follow in a mortar, rocket and/or ground attack, rules they probably never read, as the base had never had a ground attack that anyone at the Ranch had ever heard of.

As the night wore on and the hooch occupants became drunker, the language and covered wagon tales became more ribald. I was keenly aware of being the only Round Eye present and decided that the time had come to leave. The comments that greeted Bob's and my departure were in keeping with the hour and when I got to the car I decided that I would destroy some of their illusions about American girls in Vietnam as easy marks; pleading a headache (the universal female dodge), I told Bob I would drive home alone. This did not seem to upset him at all and it suddenly occurred to me – with a bit of pique – that he would probably prefer to return to the hooch and drink with his buddies, who were in fine spirits by the sounds of singing and drunken laughter rolling out into the night. I smiled to think of the flak Bob would take when he returned alone two minutes after he had left... but I felt sure his image could survive it.

I waited for him to mention another date but when he didn't, I suggested that maybe we could have that swim on Sunday that I had missed today. He concurred but with no visible enthusiasm and agreed to meet me at noon by the pool, just up the street from the hooch. As I drove away, I could hear the beginning of one of the Ranch's favorite drinking songs about an F-4 being a fat whore without a bomb door. I congratulated myself in leaving at just the right time; anything later might have cramped their style – but I doubted it.

Sunday was hot and sultry and nothing moved in the compound until about noon or so. We were still on a five-day week at that time (although I alternated Saturdays with Frenchy) and Sundays were usually devoted to recovering from hangovers – or from a Saturday trip to the commissary in Saigon – both equally debilitating. A few hardy souls jogged around the compound doing penance for the sins of the previous night, the sweat pouring off them. (I could not imagine any sin bad enough to justify such punishment.)

Just as I was getting ready to leave for the base, Sally unexpectedly showed up from Saigon. At the last minute she had hitched a ride down with some lucky Lieutenant; he was reluctant to let her go at this end but she had managed somehow to ditch him here. She said she could stay for the day then hitch a ride back with someone on the base; girls seeking rides in Vietnam never had trouble getting them (even in choppers to almost anywhere in the country).

Sally had been down for one weekend visit before and had been introduced to the Ranch Hands. Things moved fast in Vietnam, with the usual: "Be with me tonight, my darling, for tomorrow I die" – that sort of incentive. (In Vietnam, I only dated pilots and war correspondents, definitely the most interesting of the lot). On weekends we would drive over to the air base, have dinner in the Officers' Club, and then sit around drinking and talking or maybe we would pile into my VW and drive over to the Long Binh base for a pizza. On weekday mornings as I got dressed, I would often see the Ranch Hands' planes flying over the apartment on their way upcountry to defoliate; you could tell their planes even without looking by the smell of defoliant that drifted down to us. We always hoped that the same formation with the same number of planes would come back.

Yes, Sally would love to go swimming. As almost every military and USAID housing compound had a swimming pool (except for the Franzblau, alas) we often carried bathing suits with us in the hope of a cooling swim somewhere. We drove out to the air base, stopping to flirt with the MPs at the main gate; they stared bug-eyed at (now bottle-blonde) Sally who had a red, white and blue micro-mini over her bikini and looked smashing. As we went through the entrance to the American compound the guard examined our passes with interest and complained jovially about the place being overrun with women – we were the second to come to swim there in the six months he had been guarding that gate. We parked and walked to the pool entrance. I praying that Bob would be there. Sally, who was used to the Saigon scene where women were a bit more plentiful at all the swimming pools, was tugging at my shirttail and muttering under her breath:

"God, we can't go in there – there are no girls at all."

I knew the feeling, but since being in Bien Hoa I had overcome my stage fright to the point where I could brazen it out.

"Cheer up, dearie," I said condescendingly. "They're just men."

Just then, I caught sight of Bob walking towards us. I was dumbfounded: I guess I had never really looked at him very closely, other than to see that he was tall and moved well. He was not really handsome, but since his personality was so over-whelming, his looks had hardly mattered to me. Now I saw that he had a beautiful bod; broad of shoulder and narrow at the hips and with a well-knit athletic build. I must admit that for the first time he caught my full attention, which doesn't say much for my appreciation of the finer aspects of his personality and charm. I introduced him to Sally, who was also running an appraising eye over his frame. As we followed him along the side of the pool, she gave me a whispered, "He's absolutely gorgeous."

Bob returned to a table occupied by his hooch mates playing poker with kibitzers hanging around the fringes. They greeted us with appropriate enthusiasm and immediately two of the pi-lots cut Sally out of the herd and within a few minutes had her engrossed in their spiels. Bob insisted on finishing the hand, pat-ting a chair and indicating that I should sit down and shut up, which I did, grateful to sink into anonymity. The sun was blaz-ing down and the pool was filled with shouting, boisterous men. At any given moment I could tell where Sally was without even looking around; that would be the direction in which all eyes were turned, as if they were watching a ping pong match.

Bob was now discovering that he had more friends than he had thought; they came by and greeted him effusively, standing around and waiting to be introduced. But he was a past master at faking them out and he out-waited them. Very few were drawn into the inner circle by Bob and his hooch mates, who either ex-changed wisecracks or patently ignored them. The hand finished and Bob finally turned his attention to me, just as I was begin-ning to feel piqued again. He grabbed my hand and we slid into the pool; now there really was a ping pong match scenario as the eyes darted between Sally and me. Bob seemed appropriately oblivious to the stir we were causing and I had to admire his insouciance.

We had an enjoyable afternoon chatting and later playing bridge. It turned out that I was the first girl that Bob had ever dated who could play bridge – which gave a pretty good picture of the intellectual and cultural level of his former conquests. When the afternoon storm began to brew, we went down to the hooch to change into our street clothes. Someone then suggested that after dinner we go to the infamous Jupiter Club.

Since the air base belonged to the Vietnamese, the VNAF higher-ranking officers had set up some little business enterprises in shacks along the main thoroughfares: cigarette and souvenir shops, and of course numerous bars. The most elaborate of these was a palatial spread of several concrete and corrugated tin structures surrounding a covered patio and set off at some distance from the others just outside the air base near the main gate.

This was the Jupiter Club whose bar girls were reputedly better-looking and thus less hardline than those in the other bars. This plus the prime location made it the elite of the bars. I had heard about it – in fact, you could sometimes hear the blare of its music all the way down at the Franzblau – but none of my few friends or work colleagues had had the nerve to take a Round Eye there – the equivalent, I guess, of taking a ham sandwich to a banquet. Our visit there was assured when Baby Mick, the 22-year old navigator and youngest in the squadron, announced that he was going to sing with the combo that night, an announcement greeted with cheers and catcalls – as well as considerable incredulity.

Baby Mick, perhaps by virtue of his youth, was a little less practiced in holding his liquor than the others, but had been working assiduously to improve his skills that day. By the time we got ready to leave, he was in a fine fuzzy state, and the rest of the hooch crowd was not far behind him. When we finally got organized enough to make a move, we all took of for the bar on to bicycles and the more daring on locally-purchased motorcycles. We must have looked like a beginners version of a Hell's Angels ride: motorcycles weaving and bikes wobbling along in and out of everyone's path and occasionally someone just falling off the back of a moving vehicle. When we got to the Jupiter – miraculously intact – the place was swinging: several inert forms lay on benches beside the front entrance, snoring happily and illuminated by a ghastly play of alternating red and green neon lights above the entrance.

We walked by the long bar and then along the edge of the dance floor to tables located on the terrace outside since there was at least fresh air out there. The jet jockeys were already in evidence, shouting obscene and scurrilous remarks to the Ranch Hands as we entered and receiving a polite gesture of the social finger in return. We managed to commandeer a few tables and someone snagged a passing waiter and coerced him into producing some more chairs and a lot of beer. The terrace was mercifully dark so Sandy's and my presence went virtually unnoticed, except by some of the fighter pilots who started easing their way into the near vicinity.

We started dancing each time the music slowed to a danceable beat. Sally had not yet found her Man of the Hour and was playing the field, much to the delight of the guys who were sharing the wealth. As Bob and I were dancing and making snarky commentaries on our fellow dancers' styles, we were interrupted by a dashing and somewhat inebriated young man in a flight suit that indicated he was a captain and a fighter pilot. He was persistent in cutting in despite Bob's cool reception and finally Bob told me just to dance with him and get it over with; he walked off the floor, leaving me with my new dance partner.

We danced one number and I parried his questions, not difficult as his mind was considerably befuddled by booze, and then I insisted we go back to the Ranch's table when the dance was over. As we walked over, it suddenly occurred to me that this guy was just Sally's cup of tea, a party boy with a lecherous eye, and he was certainly good-looking enough to catch her attention. Sure enough, I saw in her eyes an unmistakable gleam when I introduced Robby to her. Soon their heads were together in quiet conversation and oblivious to the world around them. Baby Mick was by then well on the road to total oblivion and it was pretty obvious that he would not be singing that night after all, so Bob and I decided to cut out.

Back at the Franzblau, the Sunday evening was a lovely one for war watching from the roof. While gazing at far off flashes from mortars and the occasional arc of a rocket zooming across the distant night sky, there was time to really talk without being in the midst of a gaggle of pilots. While looking out over the air base I wondered if Bob would ever look back on his wartime flying as a pivotal point in his life (and if I would be remembered as a small part of it). I also hoped that now our budding relationship would become more normal, with less partying and drinking. The partying and drinking were soon to abate but the 'normal' was not to be, alas.

Our relationship had now begun to fall into a pattern of easy communication and comfortable mutual acceptance which is rare in new romances. I thought again of Dave, who by now seemed so remote that it was hard to imagine that I had once considered him a vital part of my life. I also wondered whether he was still in Saigon and if I would ever see him again – and if I did, how could I ever make him understand why things went wrong for us. But I put these thoughts out of my head and became totally absorbed in the here and now – and in Big Bob.

I spent most of Monday on one of the dreaded commissary

runs to Saigon and returned to the office in mid-afternoon hot, grumpy and totally exhausted. As I sat down at my desk again, Frenchy walked in with a worried expression on her face.

"Do you know someone from Saigon named Dave?"

A warning bell went off inside me.

"Sure, it's the guy I dated. He was supposed to have come over to see me here a while back but he never showed up and he never called or anything."

There was a pause as Frenchy stood silently looking down at me. At that moment I knew with sudden clarity that he was dead.

"God, Tess, I don't want to be the one to have to tell you this, but he's dead, killed by a rocket out in the province somewhere. They've been trying to get in touch with you at your old Saigon address and finally someone called and asked me to tell you, but we were cut off before we could get many details. His friend has apparently been trying to reach you for days to tell you in person. I'm sorry, I'm so damned sorry."

I just sat there uncomprehending, tears rolling down my cheeks. I had come to know death well in the last few years, having lost all of my family and two dear friends. The same numbness now overcame me – the inability to accept the fact that he was gone, vanished off the face of the earth, never to be seen by me or anyone else again. It had been easy when my mother died – my first encounter with death on a personal level – as she fell dead at my feet of a heart attack one day. Then, like her, I believed in God and in a life hereafter.

Five years later when my father died, much more slowly, I lost that belief, all on one cold February afternoon at the cemetery beside my father's grave as I stared down at the neatly cut-out oblong of earth. I suddenly knew with awful and absolute certainty that I would never see him again. His body was there under that sod but his soul, his being, was now turned off just as one turns off a light He was born, he lived his little span, and he was now gone forever. There was no way I could delude myself, at that point in time or ever, that it could be otherwise.

Now I could only weep for myself because I knew that Dave died doing the thing he believed in and loved most and in a place he chose to be. I could only hope that he died instantly, so that one minute it was all there and fine and the next minute there was nothing. Only much later did I find out (through a CIA source) that he died by an assassination and that he had lived long enough to realize all he had lost.

Frenchy asked me if I wanted to go home, but I could not bear the thought of being alone there so I worked through the long afternoon, eyes puddling behind my dark glasses, my tears sometimes falling onto the routine combat reports that I was typing.

Bob called to ask if I was coming on base to see him that night; I did not tell him what was wrong but he spotted the change in my voice – and I could only blurt out: "Please, please come over."

At the end of that long day I got home somehow and lay on my bed staring at the ceiling until Bob got there. When he walked in the door all my grief broke out in a wave of tears and I sobbed and shuddered in his comforting embrace for what must have been an hour. He then washed off my ghastly, puffy face and eyes and led me up to the roof where we watched the familiar far-off flashes and arcs. I found that every time I tried to talk the sobs broke out anew so finally we just stood silently, him patting my shoulder, his shirt front already wet with my tears. He began to talk to me quietly of war and friends and things that happen and told me I must just learn to endure – which I am still learning to do.

About curfew time, the night became relatively silent and I knew that I must face the rest of it alone. As we turned to walk down the stairs, I took one long last look at the sky. The stars were out in profusion, but there was one that was over near the horizon all alone – bigger and brighter than the rest it seemed to me – and I could say to myself, "That's Dave," and believe it. It comforted me and made the rest of the night more bearable. Bob tucked me into bed and kissed me on the forehead as I somehow drifted off into welcomed oblivion.

I got through that week somehow, working hard and for long hours and spending all my evenings quietly at home with Bob. The pattern was beginning to emerge that would characterize our future relationship. We both discovered that we preferred each other's company to always being surrounded by frenetic activity and we never seemed to run out of conversation. That week after Dave's death found me with a mixture of grief and guilt: grief because Dave was no longer in the world and guilt because I was now so content to be with Bob; he had now become my rock.

Those first weeks after our meeting and followed by the Tet offensive were critical ones in our lives. Under the stress of the new job for me and daily flying for Bob, our relationship developed much more rapidly than in perhaps a whole year of a normal friendship-to-courtship one. In reading of others who have fallen in love in wartime, this is a common theme. Daily life seems to be stripped of peripherals and one lives more intensely; the thought is always in the back of your mind that this can be taken away from you at any moment.

Bob was flying long hours, often getting up at three in the morning for a 4:15 take-off. Defoliation missions were done in two lifts – the planes having to come back to the base for another load of defoliants, and his second mission usually left about the time I was going to work. The Ranch's flights were unmistakable: four to six lumbering C-130's without identifying markings flying in close formation. Bob would tell me the night before what position he was flying and I would try to spot him every morning as he flew off to war. On the few days when there was one less plane returning than had left, I would die a thousand deaths waiting for Bob's call to tell me he was home safe. I got so well trained that I could distinguish the drone of the returning Ranch planes over the noise of the office every day.

We began to make plans for the upcoming Tet holiday. I had had only one day off from work since coming to Bien Hoa and was really looking forward to the promised two-plus day holiday (which our office would split up into shifts, since the front office always had to be covered). So at least we would have one-and-a-half days off, and if Bob could schedule his flights so that he could get the same time off, we would be able to spend it together. We debated maybe driving into the countryside and all sorts of possible alternatives but as the Tet holiday approached it looked less and less likely that our schedules would mesh.

By late January, we had decided that the best we might manage was an afternoon swim and an evening at the O Club, with a possible dinner in Saigon as an alternate plan. Our plan to maybe drive to Vung Tau now looked unlikely as we did not think we would have the time. I felt that every Vietnamese in the country would probably be on the road anyway, traveling to their homes since Tet was a combination of New Year's Eve and July 4th all rolled into one, complete with family gatherings and feasts, and of course lots of fireworks.

How prophetic that thought turned out to be.

4

TET

IN MID-JANUARY intelligence had begun to filter in suggesting that a Viet Cong attack was imminent – something Vann had long been predicting – and the pace in the office picked up. Vann was gone a lot, into Saigon for intelligence briefings or out in the field to some of III Corps' twelve provinces to talk to his men, especially in the smaller posts to check on their defensive preparations. We also set up new procedures and back-up channels for emergency communications and beefed up our sandbag emplacements around and near the office – with Vietnamese labor, of course. Any attack on Saigon would certainly include Bien Hoa and Long Binh; the capture, or at least the isolation, of these two key military bases would be critical for Viet Cong success.

It was decided that I would work the morning shift on January the 29th, the beginning of the Tet holiday, and then have the afternoon and the next day off. Sandy had also called that morning. Despite the advice to everyone in Saigon to stay put – Intelligence was still reporting the possibility of attacks somewhere in the country – she had decided to come down anyway. After all, she said, if the situation was as dangerous as everyone said it was, even despite the twenty-four hour Ceasefire that both sides had just agreed to, then it would be better to die among friends. These included her new beau, the charming jet-jockey she had recently met at the Jupiter Club. He had invited her down to join in the festivities – whatever they turned out to be – and she would be arriving at noon, this time by a chopper to land on Vann's private pad. (How she got that arranged, I dared not ask.)

I picked her up there and we went to my flat to don our most alluring dresses for meeting our sweeties at the O Club. We also were taking along our cosmetic cases so we could later "freshen up" for whatever events presented themselves – not dreaming we would still be wearing the same dresses and using those kits three days later. We also assembled emergency rations and supplies for the apartment and crisscrossed my windows with tape. The guys in the Franzblau, all of whom had weapons, had told us the day before that they had been issued extra ammo and two of them were also posted in eight-hour night shifts as look-outs on opposite corners of the Franzblau rooftop.

The Ranch Hands were in a festive mood since all their missions had been cancelled for the next twenty-four hours. The ceasefire was to go into effect at midnight, and there had been much discussion as to how we would all spend our following free days. Around 4:00 in the afternoon Bob called and said the base had just gone on "Yellow Alert", the second highest threat level of the military's gradation, indicating that an attack was imminent; now no one was allowed to leave the base. This fact did not bother Sandy and me – and certainly not the pilots.

That night – the next day would be the beginning of the Tet holiday – Sally and I dressed in our party dresses and high heels and drove over to the base for a big New Year's Eve party at the O Club. It was a little harder this time to get onto the air base, now on Alert. After some palaver, the MPs decided that while the rules said that nobody could leave the base, they did not say that nobody could come in. Smiling sweetly at the guards, we got in, I parked the car by the swimming pool, and we strolled over to the Club to meet our pilots.

We had our gala dinner and had just settled down for some celebratory champagne when the word came down that the Club was closing early. The base had now gone to Red Alert – the top category – and all its gates were now sealed. This of course meant even Sally and I could not leave, and that did not disturb the pilots unduly. As I knew, however, that base housing for the Ranch Hands was the shared hooches I had already visited, and we all knew that would not be ideal.

Our pilots left to do some backstage maneuvering and – thanks to the pull of a Master Sergeant friend of Bob's who worked in Housing Assignments – soon we were assigned to an empty VIP quarters with four beds. Our night's accommodation was nothing more than a slightly larger hooch with air conditioning, but it was far better than we had hoped for. As we went in, the guys took pains to point out where the VIP bunker was located, not that we really cared, but luckily it was just outside the door of our new home.

There was wild partying in the bar that night in a sort of "wine, dine and be merry for tomorrow we die" mood. No one really believed that an attack would come; Intelligence had been promising us a spring offensive, a summer offensive, a fall offensive and now a Tet offensive and we no longer paid much attention to their "cry wolf" alarms. The guys did insist, however, that we take certain precautions, and these only added to the suspense. They provided us with flight suits to hide the fact that we were females, an unwelcome presence on this locked-down air base, and to shield us from the dirt floor of the bunker should we ever have to use it. As Bob was over six feet tall, the crotch of my flight suit hit me at about the knees; so if any running had to be done it would be done from the knees downward only, which was going to make for some slow and picturesque movement.

We unzipped the suits and laid them on the floor beside our cots, with our shoes nearby, so that in case of an attack we would not be forced to run naked into the night. The mental picture of two naked blondes dashing out the door so enchanted the guys that they were disappointed that it was probably not to be.

We listened respectfully to their instructions, especially to the ones pertaining to bunkers: there was a VIP bunker just at our back door but that one was not to be used, as the base commander would probably be in that one and he had already voiced objections to the presence of females on his base – we were a disruptive factor in discipline and order, it seemed. (Our mental reply was that we liked to think so anyway.) To get to our bunker we were to go out to the front door and run to a bunker about fifty yards farther down the road, the one directly in front of Bob's hooch; certainly there we knew we would be a most welcomed diversion.

After much discussion the guys decided that we were too intrigued with the prospect of what the night might hold to be left alone and unwatched; they feared the danger that we might wind up in the wrong hands, i.e. not those of the VC but of their fellow pilots. Since each room had two cots – the rooms were separated by a single bath – it would be like sharing a college suite. So we said goodnight to the guys and they went over to their side, promising to free up the bathroom for us momentarily.

We talked a while about what morning might bring. Sally predicted that if an attack came in the night it would come at 3:00am but I considered that unlikely. Having had plenty to eat and drink, Sandy and I took off only our shoes and went to bed. I felt safe and secure; after all, our combat-trained pilots wouldn't let us sleep through any sort of attack, would they? I quickly dropped off to sleep.

In the middle of the night I was awakened by a distant explosion. Things were always exploding in Vietnam in those days so it didn't unduly alarm me. But then another, this one closer, and then another. I had never heard incoming mortars from any close distance but perhaps my training gleaned in those long summer afternoons watching Hollywood's B-grade war flicks had paid off; I knew instinctively that those explosions were incoming. I yelled the standard war-movie cliché, "This is it!" as I rolled out off my cot.

Sally and I hit the floor at about the same time and we heard corresponding thumps from the next room – my message had gotten through. I looked at my watch – and it was exactly 3:00am! The guys yelled for us to get into our flight suits. Sally and I fumbled to get them zipped up over our dresses – not easy when you are in a big hurry. It seemed to take an awfully long time or me to get my two legs into the suit's legs as they both seemed to want to go into only one leg or the other. But I somehow managed it and we slipped into our useless high-heel pumps – the only footwear we had – and headed for the door.

By now the noise was rolling in. It actually must have been only thirty seconds or so but we could hear the mortars "walking in", decreasing in range each time by yards as they came toward us. Now the noise was deafening and getting more so by the second; we decided this was no place for us and we should head for the bunker... fast! As we dashed past the bathroom we practically ran over our pilots heading our way – great minds were running parallel that night.

We headed out the door, me leading the pack by a length despite the handicap of the high heels. My first bound took me at least several feet down the pathway, just in time to be bowled over by the loudest noise I had ever heard. I saw orange and black and yellow flashes all intermixed somewhere behind me, but nothing else as I went flat. The hooch door had blown shut leaving the others inside and me outside alone – and suddenly very lonely. Then I heard what sounded like rain on the tin roof; it was the shrapnel falling all around me. I knew that the next incoming would surely land directly in front of me and I composed myself to die. (I remember thinking this is going to get Bob in a lot of trouble.)

Just as I had decided I was not going to wait there for Death after all, the door opened and the other three shot out at a dead run. Bob scooped me up like a football and half-dragged me toward the VIP bunker. It was apparent we were no longer going to stand on protocol – the VIP bunker was preferable to dismemberment or death. Just then there was another huge flash and a crash-bang behind the hooch we had just left. This time the noise was a bit less but it was shock waves that pounded against us. This really got us moving and we all managed to reach the bunker and dive through the entrance in a big heap – which was lucky as the next round leapfrogged over us to hit farther along on the other side of the bunker.

The bunker's sandbag walls seemed to shift a bit and smoke and cordite fumes belched through the two entrances. We all crouched together on the dirt floor, Sally and I pulling our collars up around our ears, hoping to conceal our hair, but nothing could conceal our high-heeled pumps that peeked out from beneath the legs of our flight suits. Luckily inside, there was no light except that showing through the entrances from the full moon and the flashes outside. Things boomed and heaved around us, sending sand, bugs and who knew what else, down onto us from the slightly shifting sandbags.

As the bunker began to fill up, our guys pushed us into a corner. Our two Majors turned out to be the ranking officers; they were take-charge guys anyway and they just took over. Soon they determined who had weapons – pitifully few, it turned out – and how much ammo we had in the bunker. Someone had thought to bring along the one thing we needed most: a radio that could pick up the airfield's control tower. Now we could get a running commentary on what was going on around us. As things got worse, this turned out to be a mixed blessing.

Here we were sitting in the dirt in a juddering bunker and getting a blow-by-blow description of our possible fate. Over a background of gunfire and the crash of incomings, shouts and profanity, an excited voice on the radio was yelling about Viet Cong running across the runway in our direction, then that another batch was headed toward the Headquarters building. All this was a great deal more information than I was really interested in knowing at that point. Like Woody Allen, I don't mind dying, I just don't want to be there when it happens.

Our Majors had put the two calmest armed airmen at the two bunker entrances; they had the ammo, at least a few rounds. Then we heard over the radio that the VC had crossed the runways into our area and we were sure we were goners. Sally and I both loved excitement, but this was a bit more than we had counted on. Some guys were praying, panicking, cursing, crying. (I was a little disappointed; weren't the military supposed to be the brave ones?) To our credit, Sally and I just sat quietly and waited for the end. At least we were all going to go out together, maybe in a blaze of glory just like in those B-grade movies, and not as sniveling females.

Then the attack turned as the VC headed toward the control tower. We heard machine gun fire, then a calm voice calling the shots, directing fire on them as they scuttled from one spot to another. We had apparently gotten some troops into the fight, so now we might prevail after all. As the VC had relied on surprise and speed rather than masses of troops, that is where we had the advantage. Things then began to quiet down outside and inside the bunker. Cigarettes were lit, somebody said something funny and we all laughed in relief as we realized that we were probably going to live through the night after all.

Our pilots, finally remembering that we were there, came over and checked that we were both OK. Bob patted me on the head and said, "Good girl". The control tower spotter's voice was now more like that of a sports' announcer, pointing out a bit of action here, a bit there. There were no more screams and curses, no more big explosions, just a smattering of small arms fire.

In our little corner, we would probably have gone undetected had not some idiot lost something he wanted to look for. Using a cigarette lighter for illumination he slowly moved through the bunker searching the ground. We were hunched down, leaning against the bunker's sandbags and we put our heads down on our knees, as if asleep, and hoped we had gone undetected. He did not pause as the light passed over us, but when he returned to the other end of the bunker there was mumbling and whispering, and the curses and obscenities that had filled the air now ceased. Bob kept watch at the entrance as the sound of small-arms fire began in the far distance. Then the All-Clear sounded and we exited hastily, having no desire to converse with the base commander in case he came to check his VIP bunker.

It was now light outside so we decided to return to the hooch. It was still standing but the sides were riddled with shrapnel and the door was blown open. Inside, there was also shrapnel and I found a jagged piece lying on my bed. I saved it for years as a reminder to myself of what I might have gotten in my quest for an exciting life. All the ceiling's light fixtures were hanging only by their electric cords. A large shard of metal had come through the wall about an inch above the beds and apparently ricocheted off the bedside table, leaving a long gouge in it. In general, however, the hooch was in far better shape than we expected since luckily it had been bracketed rather than hit by mortar rounds.

We discovered later that the round that had first knocked me to the ground had demolished an officer's trailer on the far side of our hooch but had been partially absorbed by that other bunker, thus saving us. We gathered up our scattered possessions and debated what we would do next. We were so relieved to be alive that we were in high old spirits – our adrenalin was still pumping and I felt a great surge of vitality and nervous energy. We sobered up slightly when we looked out the hooch door to see flames in the vicinity of the swimming pool. I had left my car parked there and it suddenly occurred to me that I probably no longer had a car.

Except for occasional bursts of machine gun fire in the far distance, things seemed to have returned to something approaching normal. Phones began to ring and a loudspeaker blared directing all airmen to report to their units. Our guys parked us in the O Club, which was just beginning to serve strong coffee, and told us to stay put. Not that we had a choice; no one was allowed onto or off the base, an order that was to continue for several more days. Sally and I did eventually venture out to walk over to the swimming pool to see what had happened to my little VW. There it sat in the brilliant moonlight, absolutely untouched. We walked around it and could not find even a single nick in the paint. It too led a charmed life.

I learned that night a great deal more about mortars than I really wanted to know. I learned that you can sometimes mistake outgoing for incoming – but that you never make a mistake on the incoming. I learned that mortars and rockets are primarily anti-personnel weapons. I still had in mind the scenes of destruction I had seen in Berlin after World War II: whole blocks of houses gone, leveled by a single raid or an artillery barrage. Here, mortars had hit the concrete runways, but instead of making gaping craters, they had merely chipped the surface a bit as all of the force was funneled outward and upward. I heard of men who had mortar and rocket rounds hit right beside where they were crouched or lying and, although considerably shaken, they were not hurt, while a friend standing upright some yards away was hit by the metal. I learned to distinguish between .88 and 1.22mm mortars, the latter much more noisy and devastating. I learned that the actual noise level was the one thing the war movies could not capture – at least not without hurting the eardrums of the audiences.

The whole sequence I had been through seemed as familiar to me as if I had been through it many times before – and yet, barring possible reincarnation, I had never before heard a shot fired in anger. The sirens even sounded exactly like the ones that sounded in London during the blitz – but I suppose that wail is a universal sound and not exclusive to any particular place. I learned that once the initial terror of the unknown is over, the adrenalin takes over and it is then exciting and not particularly scary – in fact, I don't remember being afraid after that first few minutes that night. But maybe one just forgets the fear?

I also discovered that once you have the fear factor licked, you can assess the odds of your dying or being wounded. And I suspect it is so much easier to overcome fear in an impersonal mortaring or rocketing, since the odds of your getting killed are infinitesimally small. After all, one of the things that had brought me to Vietnam was my theory that the odds of me – or any female – getting killed in Vietnam were almost nil. And hadn't I just proved it?

We walked over to the Ranch where we found groups of jubilant Ranch Hands; everyone had emerged unscathed that night – except for a captain who tried to run right through a motor scooter and only succeeded in fighting it to a standstill. But it

TET

so slowed his progress that instead of diving in the bunker entrance as planned, he dived six inches wide of it and rammed his head into the wooden support frame, receiving a mild concussion from that and multiple cuts and bruises from the motor scooter. As it occurred during a rocket account, this technically made him a war casualty, although whether he later received a Purple Heart for it we never learned.

The combat stories grew wilder – and even less credible – as the drinks flowed freely. Everyone had his story and it soon became a can-you-top-this contest. Just as our little clique was about to toss yet another tale into the ring, the sirens went off again and the group scattered like buckshot. Although Bob had just finished complaining how his back had reacted badly to the last headlong flight, he now passed me with the speed of a gazelle. (He claimed he was not running but had passed several guys who were.) We all jammed up in the entrance to the bunker and wound up in a heap inside as the familiar sound of the incoming mortars walked toward us.

This time, however, they seemed to be concentrated on the area of the runways that lay about a quarter mile from the Ranch. About six fell within a few seconds of each other and then there was a long silence. Then a single round fell a great deal closer to us. Our current bunker held EMs (Enlisted Men) and a few Ranch Hand officers and they were definitely not timid about expletives. The air was blue with words (that I hadn't known existed until I read *From Here to Eternity*), with an occasional "'scuse me, ma'am" after a particularly colorful outburst.

This bunker was smaller than the other one and we sat all jammed up together, hugging our knees and trying to get smaller. As the noise abated we gradually relaxed, the boys moving away to clear a space for Sally and me to stretch our legs. Bob was complaining loudly that he was going to have to be carried out of the bunker and put in traction – that his back was truly broken this time. When I mentioned his gazelle-like speed he denied it hotly, maintaining that he had crawled to the bunker all the way on his hands and knees. He was a very funny guy.

Baby Mick had had the presence of mind to grab a half-full bourbon bottle on the way to the bunker; it was now empty and he was sitting upright in a corner and smiling dreamily, his expression showing a total lack of concern for his surroundings. Someone peeped out the entrance and reported no visible hostile activity, and after a brief discussion it was decided that the VC were through for now. We had no more than come to this conclusion than there was a sharp burst of automatic rifle fire, alarmingly close from the sound of it. Machine guns and BAR's began to chatter and our armchair strategists starting making quick reassessments; I saw one guy furtively cross himself – not a reassuring sight.

Our enterprising airman had again brought his radio tuned in to the tower frequency, the control tower being less than half a mile away. We soon learned that both ends of the runway were under attack, the VC had penetrated the perimeter despite the heavy minefield that was supposed to make it impossible. We were to find out later that the damp ground had defused all the mines. I was glad we did not know that night that all that separated our bunker from the base perimeter was a road, a field, some concertina and the useless minefield.

We again inventoried the weapons we had in the bunker: only one, a .45 service revolver with a single clip of ammo. Someone dashed out and came back with two M-16s and a cartridge belt – not exactly enough to make us a fortress, but certainly a decided improvement.

The tower radio was again supplying a running commentary on the progress of the battle, which would have been entertaining if the situation had not been so critical. We heard the sound of aircraft circling the field, trying to get permission to land. The tower kept saying "do not land, our runways are under fire or "those guys you see on the runway are not, repeat not, friendly forces, and the runways are not secure".

There was some haggling about where to go, and the tower rather sarcastically suggested that any place might be better than here. We then learned that Tan Son Nhut Airfield in Saigon was also under attack; pilots had been turned away from there and were now running out of fuel. Some tower wag suggested that Hanoi might be the only place in Vietnam that not was not under attack right now, but I noted that nobody laughed.

The staccato fire continued and now new firing began to come from another direction, this time farther off. We all turned expectantly to the radio. As if at a Sunday afternoon football game within a minute we had our update – it was at the main gate; the one we used to enter the base was now being attacked by a squad of VC. I could only imagine the fear of the young MPs guarding the gate (their ranks now supplemented, we hoped, by US or ARVN defenders).

We had gotten to know most of the MPs as they were always friendly (and flirty to us girls) and slightly in awe of Bob, whose comings and goings hinted at a high life they could not hope to experience. Now there were frantic calls for any lightships (helicopters fitted with huge searchlights that could focus directly on the attackers) in the area to help repel the attack there. The air was then filled with the sounds of choppers "hosing down" – their machine guns make a brrrrrrrrrppppppp sound like the tearing of a gigantic sheet – followed by a deadly silence. I assumed all the choppers were either down refueling or had gone off to fight elsewhere. The firing continued sporadically for a bit, but soon everything became totally quiet, actually scarier than the noisy part because maybe the gate had been breached? We had no idea.

Would we ever see our young friends again? After what seemed like a lifetime, but was perhaps no more than five minutes, we again heard the sound of choppers and the man at the bunker entrance reported that flares were being dropped in the gate area. At about 4:00am the firing ceased in the direction of the runways and the tower reported no new activity. The VC had either been repelled or had withdrawn from the action to fight another day, one of their most crafty and successful strategies. Around 4:30, the all-clear sounded and we emerged from the stuffy smoke-filled bunkers into a cool sparkling morning. As I breathed in deep drafts of fresh air, I suddenly felt weary but peaceful. We had lived to see the dawn of a new day, but the process had taken a lot out of us. We dragged ourselves back to the Ranch and all collapsed onto every available bed and chair. I think we all were asleep within five minutes.

Our rest turned out to be short-lived; the field phone soon began to ring calling all the Ranch Hands down to Ops for an emergency meeting. There was much groaning and hawking and spitting but finally the inanimate lumps began to move and the hooch was soon empty. Sally and I used this opportunity to freshen up, which consisted primarily of sneaking into the empty latrine to wash some of the grime off our faces and bods. We then again flopped down on now-empty cots and slept soundly until the guys returned around noon.

By now the base was really getting organized: trucks rumbled up and down the roads dropping huge loads of sand at intervals, followed by another truck from which empty sandbags were tossed. The order was now out that all bunkers were to be reinforced by at least one added layer of sandbags and work was to start on sandbagging the sides of all the hooches to waist level.

Bob brought the news that another sector of the base had been hit; the side containing the flight mechanics and flight-line personnel had taken a direct hit, killing men as they emerged from their bunker. There were nine other assorted casualties, some of them quite serious.

One of the first men killed had been the bookkeeper at the NCO club; he was counting the night's receipts upstairs over the club when a mortar had come through the roof, killing him instantly but not even touching the man standing near him. This confirmed once more my fatalistic feeling that there was no point in trying to run away from random danger – there was really no one place safer than any other. But I noted that sandbags were being filled with great enthusiasm, each hooch fielding a crew of dedicated workers. Only much later did they initiate the practice of hiring Vietnamese women to fill the bags at so much per hour, with payment being made from the hooch slush funds. You had to admire American ingenuity – or laziness.

The guys had all been issued additional weapons and ammo, and stockpiles of it were being placed at strategic locations around the base. Sally and I found our afternoon's work cut out for us when it was discovered that the M-16 ammunition clips were so old they were clogged with dirt and each clip had to be emptied and the bullets polished one by one. Several officers came back from a quick trip to the firing range to report that the malfunction rate of the M-16's they fired was one in three. I had heard the frequent complaint in Vietnam that the M-16 could be relied upon to jam or misfire when you really needed it, but now it became a matter of personal concern and before the afternoon was over, I found myself getting quite angry – angry that some DOD contract might be the cause of some of my friends getting killed.

Weaponry now became the source of some ardent attention;

officers who had not touched carbines since basic training suddenly became enthusiastic students of anyone with slightly more expertise than they. The .45 service revolvers that they all carried when flying were said to be so inaccurate that it was debated whether a man would even be able to commit suicide with it – if aimed in his ear it was just as likely to shoot down a passing bird.

Bob appointed himself hooch honcho and we had a summit conference. It was decided that the four hooch mates of the OK Corral would be responsible for the defense of the bunker directly in front of the hooch – the one in which we had spent the latter part of the night – with one man assigned to each door. The EM's had not yet been issued weapons, so the armament would consist of an M-16 with ten extra clips for each of the four officers, plus assorted .45's, and whatever else could be dug up, including souvenir ChiCom (Chinese Communist) rifles and even a Czech-made AK-47 – the most respected small arms weapon in Vietnam, but one unfortunately issued only to the VC.

Sally's jet jockey had been called back to his squadron early that morning and from our vantage point on top of a bunker we watched the base's choppers zooming around all day. Sally was fretting about him and I was rather antsy from lack of sleep myself, so Bob kept us busy with little chores all day long. There was still fighting all around the base and another onslaught at its perimeters was still a possibility. We could see in the distance black smoke still billowing up from a fire in a petrol dump somewhere. There was reportedly still fighting in the streets and it was rumored that snipers were being rooted out of the Bien Hoa Club, a four-story structure a block from the Franzblau. I suspected this might be true since it commanded an excellent view of the main gate of the III Corps Headquarters that housed a lot of ARVN officers and some American advisors. Word had already come down that they had three KIA (killed in action) there and that there was now street-by-street clearing of the area directly across from the gate – which meant that they were now fighting on both sides of the Franzblau.

It was impossible to get through to the office, but no one was allowed to leave the base under any circumstances so that took care of that problem. I regretted momentarily that I was missing a piece of the action but I knew they would have herded the women off somewhere for safety anyway; at least on the base we were put to work and could make ourselves useful, if only to make the officers feel more protective and gallant by our presence.

Bob took Sally and me aside and showed us how the cartridge clips worked. He wanted us to stand behind him and the man at the other bunker entrance and feed them the clips as they expended them in firing. I'm sure he felt that by keeping us busy during any future fighting he would prevent panic and also would be able to keep an eye on us. I was touched by his well-intended concern and decided not to point out to him that Sally and I had been by far the calmest in the recent action. I guess it was a case of "where ignorance is bliss," but Sally and I still regarded the whole affair as rather wearing but very exciting. Neither she nor I lost this cavalier attitude until much later, when we were worn down by constant night mortaring and lack of sleep and when we began to realize that friends who were gone were not gone just for the duration of the war.

But that day, we were in our element: busy, useful (or so we imagined) and happily pig-dirty. Bob finally got back to us and suggested we go up to the men's locker room at the swimming pool – closed because of the flak in it – and take a shower while he stood watch. I suggested he take his carbine with him, for if word spread that there were two naked Round Eyes in the bath house he would have to fight off the troops. He found my quip

unfunny but relented and put up elaborate OFF LIMITS TO ALL
EXCEPT FEMALE PERSONNEL signs; this of course connoted
hordes of women using the facility, and any patient onlookers
must have been keenly disappointed at the sight of only two
grubby strays emerging during the whole day.

None of the Vietnamese employees had been allowed on base
that morning so any service facilities dependent on them were
shut down. The O Club was serving sandwiches only and a field
kitchen had been set up as a messing facility – nobody seemed
to be too hungry anyway. After we had gotten squeaky clean,
Bob consented to take us to the O Club so that Sally could search
for any officers from the fighter squadron and find out how and
where her pilot was, as all the phones on that side of the base
were out.

The first person we saw when we walked in was the base commander who immediately approached us in a very determined
manner. At that moment, I was more scared than I had been all
night – would he throw us off the base or just court martial Bob?
He certainly knew by now that we had been there all night –
our haggard looks proved that if nothing else did. He came up
to us and grabbed both Sally and me by the hand: Had we got
any rest? Were we all right? Did we need anything? His concern
seemed genuine and, turning to Bob he told him we were not
to be allowed off-base until the town was again declared safe.
He would find suitable housing for us somewhere in the Ranch
area. Bob told him that was taken care of and he didn't question
it further, which was fortunate since I don't think he would have
considered sleeping in the OK Corral with Bob and three other
pilots "suitable" housing. I'm sure he knew the score, but he did
not wish to be told. In any event, Sally and I went limp with relief
and managed to mumble our thanks. We sensed he would become more hostile again later – which, incidentally he did – but

today, he was all for protecting American Womanhood.

Sally's pilot then got word to her that he was alive and well and busy with air strikes but would find her as soon as he was free – and in the meantime, we were to stay out of the clutches of those "goddam Ranch Hand Romeos." Bob sent back word that she was well taken care of – and frequently – and to bring more booze when he came because the Ranch was running out. We all ate and went back to the hooch for another catnap. The atmosphere was now more relaxed – everyone felt more secure, as "probably" the worst was over.

About 7:00pm, we suited up again, this time with flight suit leg pockets crammed with extra ammo clips, flashlights, pocket knives and military paraphernalia until our shins were black and blue just from walking with the load. I shuddered to think of how we would beat ourselves to death if we ever had to run. The evening news made vague references to fighting all over Vietnam, which brought forth catcalls and cries of "no shitting!" On AFN (the American Forces Network) even when we could see Saigon being rocketed they did not reveal that to us.

Someone brought over a case of Cokes and we all sat around on the lawn chewing the fat and watching the varied, and sometimes humorous, preparations for the night. Some enterprising EMs were already lugging mattresses into the bunkers – and had to be told to lug them back out again as they were taking up too much space.

The entrance to the bunker had now been re-sandbagged to form a protected position from which weapons could be fired. Then we watched with disgust as a huge dump truck proceeded to drive too close to it and knocked the whole thing down. The rebuilding occupied some time, especially since there were ten versions of how it should be done to every one bag actually lifted into place. The finished product finally approved, someone then noted that in order to enter the bunker at any speed beyond crawling it would be necessary to negotiate an S-turn in single file – or else dive over it, but in single file too, please.

Bob and his hooch mates were keeping an eagle eye on one special corner of the bunker where they had stashed a supply of booze for "medical purposes". The pilots all had their flak jackets with them, and each person had a little pile of possessions that he meant to carry into the bunker. (At eight o'clock when the siren went off,` most of the possessions got left behind.)

The transition from the picnic-like atmosphere to the war was instantaneous: all grabbed weapons and dashed into the bunker, predictably tripping over the sandbag entrance barrier and crawling, cursing, into the bunker. I cleared the distance in about three leaps, banging my shins and dragging my flak vest behind me. (It proved much too heavy to wear but was great for lying on, thus protecting you somewhat from the dirt floor.) But it was Long Binh's night for the mortars and rockets and we could hear them getting hit, although it was some five miles away.

There was sporadic fire on our base perimeter but nothing really close and soon almost everyone was sleeping, their snores rending the stale bunker air. Bob and I finally crawled outside and lay on our flak vests in the ditch that had been dug around the bunker. The stars were out big and bright and planes crisscrossed over our heads, sometimes dropping illuminating flares that cast an eerie white light over the countryside. We discussed all the things we both wanted to do if we survived the war, for there was no doubt in our minds that this was the beginning of the real war in Vietnam and we both had nearly a year left on our tours.

Men were now sneaking back into their hooches and sacking out, or carrying ice and cups back to the bunker; some merely sprawled out on the ground, snoring happily until rudely awakened by the MPs. Around 5:00am, the all-clear finally sounded and a loudspeaker truck drove slowly through the compound telling everyone to return to his hooch and await further instructions. Once again the OK Corral looked like a Greyhound Bus Terminal, with people asleep on every available horizontal surface. Bob's hooch seemed to always have "house guests" for some reason, whether because of the company or the booze, I don't know.

Bob gave Sally and me the cots in the back room: One was notable for the lovely lacey 32-C bra pinned over it, supposedly taken off a Donut Dolly (Red Cross volunteer) without her even missing it, and Bob's for the white silk parachute in which he always wrapped himself at night. He said it felt just like women's panties and aided his sleep immeasurably, to say nothing of his dreams. His hooch mates all scoffed but Bob noted that every time they went by his bed they reached down and caressed the silk lovingly; he was thinking of charging 25 cents a feel just to pay for the wear and tear. After a few hours of blissful sleep the phones began to ring again and Tet+3 was underway.

That day was spent mostly alone as the military had far more important things to do than attend to us. We were getting antsy and wanted to get back to our apartments – and of course to notify everyone that we were all right. I should have known that Vann would soon start missing me – he had things to do and I was part of his backup team. Sure enough, one of the first messages to get through to us was a curt one from him.

He had somehow tracked me down – his spies were everywhere, he claimed – demanding that we "get the Hell back to work and quit malingering with the goddamned pilots". Further, even if the Air Force could sleep till noon, he had a war to fight out there and all his secretaries – except Frenchy who was pissed off to be missing the fun – were shacked up on the air base. I pointed out with great dignity that we had just spent two sleepless nights in a bunker, but I promised that I would be in to work the next day even if I had to crawl under the concertina barbed wire to get off the base. He said he would send Colonel Wilson over that night to get us.

The guys were horrified to think of us going off the base alone and unprotected, but Sally and I were getting curious as to what life was like on the outside and more than a little eager to change into some fresh clothes. When Bob saw that we really were going to leave he objected, pointing out the hazards and calling Vann a few colorful names for requiring us to leave our secure position; it did not appease him much when I pointed out that mortaring and ground fighting nightly did not exactly insure our on-base security; what worse could happen anywhere else, f'gawdsake?

Colonel Wilson apparently drove his white Ford up to the gate and demanded to get in to pick us up. He was told that the base was locked down. Colonel Wilson was an imposing military figure even in civilian clothes, erect and steely-eyed, and he was not noted for his patience. I'd have to guess at what he said to the MPs but whatever it was it got him inside the gate in a matter of seconds. He also demanded that they open the security barriers and keep them open until he returned – something that worried them a great deal but they did it. Sally and I got in the car and sat quiet as little mice in the back seat and as the car drove out the gate, the MPs were like ants scurrying back with their displaced materials and rapidly reestablishing their old barriers.

As we drove out the gate, a nervous MP volunteered the information that we should not turn left – "They've been firing at us from there". Colonel Wilson just grunted, and immediately turned left.

The streets of Bien Hoa were empty and eerily quiet. As we passed the gas station on the corner, we could see the shell of the burned-out portion. We were the only car on the road and I felt very much like a duck in a shooting gallery. As we approached the Franzblau gate Colonel Wilson turned on the inside light so that we could be clearly visible to the Vietnamese gate guards. At least they were supposed to be at the gate, but it took several honks of the horn to bring one into sight.

The gate slowly swung open to reveal a different Franzblau from the one we had left only a few days before. Some of the windows now had clear plastic stretched across the openings. Sandbags formed barricades across each apartment building entrance and trigger-happy civilians with high-powered weaponry crouched behind them, every rifle pointed at us. I soon learned that everyone in Vietnam, whether he had even a nodding acquaintance with his weapon or not, kept it not only loaded but also chambered – a thought not designed to give one much peace of mind in a compound of eighty tenants, and probably double that number of weapons.

Colonel Wilson deposited us at the entry door and told me that I'd be picked up for work the next morning. In my apartment I had expected shambles but found not even a window broken. By being on the ground floor and the back side of the building, we were partially protected by the high compound wall. I felt that the reports of extensive damage in the area of the Franzblau must have been exaggerated. Even the dust in my apartment was unmoved.

Sally and I took two showers each and fell into our beds between clean sheets, sighing at the sheer bliss of it. We slept the sleep of the innocent. At least we did until 6:30am when the sound of choppers taking off roused us straight up from our beds, wild-eyed and grabbing for our flight suits. By the time we realized where we were and that we were not being mortared – had we slept through an attack we wondered – we were wide awake, so we decided to go up to the roof and greet the dawn.

As we walked to the railing we both simultaneously gasped. Almost all the densely-populated houses next door to us were gone. In their place were heaps of burned timbers and shattered stucco blackened and ventilated by large and small holes. As I leaned out over the railing to look down on the little Buddhist temple which lay just outside the compound wall, I saw that a few buildings closest to the wall were still standing. In the small temple courtyard in the dim morning light, I could see a robed monk prostrating himself and then rising and bowing. An old woman was placing incense sticks in a large iron pot of sand at one side. The contrast between the destruction around it and the tranquility of the temple brought tears to my eyes.

I looked around the roof. Sandbags blocked off each corner and field telephone wires were strung from one corner to the other. Several Vietnamese and American guards dozed in their corners, weapons across their knees. They looked so tired that we moved quietly out of earshot to carry on our conversation, looking out over the air base that had until so recently been our refuge. Would they ever let us back on it again? We had tried to call the Ranch upon our return the night before, but the phones were out so we could only imagine what the guys were thinking. Sally promised to keep trying to contact them when I went to work and I was to inquire about possible connections to Saigon – if indeed there were any. She did manage later to reach her office and was told to just stay put at the Franzblau; this was welcomed as we had not talked ourselves out.

When I got to the office, the bosses were out somewhere in the province and I had a surprisingly quiet day. The military was still not moving around much so we had few visitors and the phones must still have been down. We would occasionally hear a vehicle screech to a halt outside and the door would burst open as a soldier dashed in. He almost invariably was wearing a flak jacket and helmet and with rifle in hand. (Since I had been ferried to work that morning in an open jeep, I felt this was a bit much.) We even had trouble getting them to put down their weapons while talking to us; they had a tendency to want to hang on to them even when they went to the latrine. We finally had to make a rule that all weapons had to be cleared before entering the building, or else we would probably have gotten our heads blown off. Other than those few minor changes, the office seemed much the same, only now less busy.

That would certainly change when everyone got back from the field and started reporting; many busy days obviously lay ahead. But when I asked for a few hours off to go back to the air base to retrieve my car, it was granted. With Sally not yet needed in Saigon and the air base reported as now secured, we thought we could nip over, pick up my car, maybe say hello to our pilots, and drive back. The office even gave me an official car and driver to take us on to the base; Headquarters motor pool was definitely not busy if it could do that for us.

Sally and I had no problem getting on the base in a government car and asked the driver to just take us to the Ranch to give back our flight suits and we would walk to the car. Alas, Bob must have been flying, but two of the Ranch Hands I did not know (but who knew us!) were happy to accompany us to the swimming pool where my VW still sat. We climbed in and waved gaily at our two well-wishers. I'll admit I did feel like I was leaving the old homestead as we drove off, skirting mounds of sand and sandbags.

We started to drive toward the main gate and had no more than cleared the Ranch cantonment area and moved out past the open fields than we were halted by MPs who informed us that the road leading to the main gate was now closed. There were

still some VC in the field by the perimeter road and the GIs who
had been called in as a reaction force that morning were in the
process of rounding them up. Far off, we could see them moving
in the high brush along the perimeter road. We then decided we
would make a run for it by means of a shortcut down through
the hanger area and along the flight line. I made a sharp left and
headed for the runways. As we meandered along, we discovered that we weren't quite as sure of our way as we had thought
and there were all sorts of new barriers now to be skirted that
made us lose our sense of direction. We drove around for a while
wondering why there were no people around. We finally got out
of the hanger area and headed toward what we hoped was the
main gate. But the more we drove, the more lost we got.

We finally turned a corner and there was a whole army camp
spread out in front of us – sprung up overnight like mushrooms. By now, there was quite a bit of small arms fire in the
distance. There were at least troops in the camp, but they were
all crouched down behind sandbag barriers. An officer ran back
and forth yelling orders. We beeped our horn for attention, not
wishing to get out of the car and interrupt anything, especially if
it was something essential like fighting. We were totally ignored,
so we beeped again. A soldier then looked back over his shoulder and did a classic double-take upon seeing two Round Eyes
in a Volkswagen signaling him over. He nudged his buddy who
also turned and stared slack-jawed. The first guy ran over to us,
keeping his head down and looking nervously over his shoulder.
When he got to the car he squatted down beside it and looked up
at us inquiringly.

"We're sorry to bother you, but could you tell us the way to
the main gate?"

He stared, bug-eyed, and remained silent a moment. He then
motioned to his friend.

"Hey, Joe, come over here a minute – you ain't gonna believe this!"

Joe came zig-zagging over and crouched beside the car.

"They wanna know the way to the main gate."

Joe's mouth fell open as he gazed into the car. "You gotta be shittin' me, lady!"

We explained patiently that we were trying to leave the base but we were lost, that's all. When they had pulled themselves together, they informed us that there was at that moment a firefight with some VC over in the field and that the whole base was on alert. Hadn't we heard the sirens? Nooooo, but we had noticed no one was moving except us. Well, at least that explained why we had not found anyone to ask directions.

"But what the hell are you doing here?" As an afterthought he added, "ma'am".

"We are trying to go home as soon as we can find the main gate," I patiently explained.

"Hell, we thought you was on a Sunday afternoon drive. Are you-all crazy... ma'am?"

Just then, there was the sound of gunfire in the distance that flattened both of them to the ground where they lay peeping up from under their helmets like beached turtles. It was Sally's and my turn to stare. We found it rather off-putting to try to carry on a conversation with two men lying on the ground with their heads almost underneath the running board. We definitely sensed that our presence made them uncomfortable so we excused ourselves politely and asked them to move their heads, and yes, we would be able to find the gate all right, thank you, and no we wouldn't dream of lying down on the dirt and besides, we didn't think the bullets were very close, were they?

This exchange reduced them to slack-jawed immobility again so we just eased around them and then roared off, heading toward what surely must be the perimeter road again. We finally hit it at a recognizable spot and headed toward the gate with the road all to ourselves as we drove along. We chatted about the new Army guys we had just seen. We decided somebody must have pushed the panic button as it didn't look to us all that threatening. As we came to a familiar spot where the MPs usually directed traffic, we at first saw nobody. Then a closer inspection revealed an arm rising out of a ditch and motioning us to halt. We stared in fascination at the disembodied member which gradually rose to reveal a head with a white MP helmet attached to it, screaming, "We're in cross-fire! Get down get down!"

So that's what those funny pings were that we had been hearing (I had thought it was from the motor), sounds that were not audible or threatening from inside a sealed car with a noisy motor. With the window open, we could now hear an occasional thud. This really caught our attention; we realized it was the sound of a bullet impacting in the ground or on some object. Since we didn't want the object to be our bodies, we took Waving Arm's advice with alacrity and zoomed off at right angles and headed back toward the hanger area. Nobody had to tell us to hurry at this stage – faster than a speeding bullet (we hoped), we zoomed down the road we had just come along, leaving the noise behind us.

As we slowly drove back beside the runway along the parked airplanes we saw an Air Force jeep coming our way, a determined looking officer at the wheel. What the hell were we doing there, and where were we headed? We explained to the Colonel, trying to make it sound official, that we had been instructed to return to the Ranch cantonment area at once. He just shook his head in disgust and told us to follow him and not to stop for anything until we got to our destination; we were screwing up things in the control tower and on the flight line.

I conjured up a vision of what we must have looked like from the tower: a little white beetle playing beneath the feet of elephants. We smiled sweetly and followed him back to the Ranch area. When we finally drove up to the OK Corral and honked the horn, Bob shot out of the door, cursing Sally and me in his first breath. When he saw the Colonel, he stopped short and saluted smartly.

The Colonel was brisk and brief: "If these young ladies belong to you, Major, I suggest you keep your eye on them. Every time I look up I see them going by in one direction or another. And I've seen a great deal more of them today than I really want to."

I thought I noted a twinkle in his eye but I couldn't swear to it. Bob promised that we would be under his direct surveillance and would cause no more trouble with our meanderings. He said, with a great deal of satisfaction, that we would not be allowed out of his sight again. After the colonel left, Bob spent five minutes in a diatribe about what idiots we were. I was rather hurt by his attitude until Little Mick took me aside and told me that Bob had been really worried when he had heard that we were coming to retrieve my car, and then heard the firing on the other side of the base. He had kept repeating over and over, "I knew this would happen, I just knew it!"

Sally and I sat contritely for a bit while he poured himself a drink and we explained how we really had not been in any danger – it only looked that way from this side of the base, etc etc. He remained unconvinced but finally mellowed to the point where he could share our escapades with a visiting Ranch Hand (there always seemed to be visitors when we were there). He recounted our escapades with gusto, interspersed with much grumbling about "damfools" and "idiots".

I knew Bob wanted us to stay on for an extended conversation and maybe some drinking and I decided we had to get out of there now despite his continued protests. I babbled something bright and inane about how we had been gone too long and were awaited at the office and really must go now. Sally then rose and in a burst of creativity stated she knew I had promised to go back to the office immediately after picking up my car and we were already late and Bob didn't want to get me in trouble, did he? He acquiesced but insisted on driving with us until we got onto the main road leading directly to the gate, as he could not trust me not to screw it up again. I thanked him profusely for 'saving us' by assuring that we would not get lost and we all headed out. As we drove (once again) near the perimeter road, I did wonder if the VC had ever been flushed out of the field on our left.

With the gate in sight, Bob bailed out and we agreed I would come back onto the base the coming weekend if things remained quiet. He kissed me goodbye, but was still grumbling about our folly as he started his return walk to the Ranch. I got us off the base and back to the office in record time, only to be told that since it was still quiet and I had a Saigon visitor – I had introduced Sally around and she had charmed everyone – I should just go home. We left with alacrity before they changed their minds, and spent our probable last evening recounting to each other the highlights of a very adventurous few days. Sally agreed that Saigon was going to seem pretty tame from now on, and promised to come down to see me (and of course her pilot) as often as she could get away.

The next morning when we woke up and made our rooftop survey of the air base, the perimeter nearest us had become a beehive of activity, with troops, tanks and helicopters amidst sandbagged machine gun posts. All around us was devastation. The VC had apparently come in, or possibly out, via the back of the Franzblau, but our compound's high concertina-topped walls had remained unbreached; we were obviously not their target. Sally had arranged a ride to Saigon and we said goodbye as we took off to our respective posts. I worked for days and days almost without a break. Things had now begun 'hotting up' again and my job was made harder because the CIA – yes, they were there in our headquarters too – had sent all its female personnel to Saigon for safety as soon as the Yellow Alert had been announced, while our USAID gals had stayed put. We were either tougher, or were simply expendable. (A CIA guy later gave me a nifty camera as thanks for doing his evacuees' work.)

We saw little of Vann in the immediate aftermath of Tet. When he was not up in Saigon for meetings he spent most of his days choppering from outpost to outpost, province to province, checking on his men, propping up ARVN officers and spotting holes in defense measures, doing what he did best: leading and inspiring. We talked to him a lot on the field phone, taking orders and relaying them down the pipeline. He would pop in, shouting instructions as he came through the door, and then he was gone again – his chopper hardly ever cooled off. Colonel Wilson kept the office running and we never let them down. If we had, we would have been out of there, trust me.

There continued to be occasional rocket attacks on and around Bien Hoa. In the Franzblau, we first upended our beds to form blast shields and slept on mattresses on the floor, sheltered by all that teakwood, but after a few days of no hits nearby we got pretty blasé. The twin beds returned to upright but I did keep a mattress on the floor beside my bed so that if something hit close I could just roll off the bed onto it and then go right back to sleep. If the rockets came early on a beautiful evening, I would go sit on the roof and listen to them as they zoomed over, high above and hitting with a brief flash far in the distance. There were still guys up there behind sandbags at night but it was now infiltration and sabotage that was feared, not further ground attacks.

The watch standers told me about one of our USAID guys, a Texan who was always trumpeting his desire to fight the "gooks" rather than do whatever he was assigned (it was in an agriculture project, as I recall). He always swaggered around with a pair of pistols on his hip, swathed in double bandoliers of ammo. (Who ever needed two? Except maybe on the first night of Tet, as it turned out.) We all considered him a real phony and Tet had proved us to be right: He had been assigned to rooftop duty on the first post-Tet night. Not only had he not shown up for his shift but he had just disappeared! Later we learned that he had somehow gotten to Saigon, caught the first flight out, returned to Texas, and from there sent a telegram to USAID saying that he was resigning because of ill health. Yeah, we said, a problem with his guts.

Tet was the last big fight for me but I was to have a few more minor attention-grabbing incidents. On a solo trip to the base somewhat later, I was driving my VW along and listening to AFN on the radio when I saw guys in trucks and jeeps in front of me bailing out and diving into a nearby ditch. I remember that I was wearing one of my favorite dresses, a white one, and I most certainly was not going to dirty that dress. I opened the car door and sort of crouched down beside it.

I heard no sound of firing, I have no idea why, but did hear around me a series of clicks, a rather odd, different kind of sound. There were shouts of "Get down, get down!", so I gingerly lowered myself onto a bit of grass I had spotted on the bank of the dirty ditch. It turned out that a few VC had somehow managed to dig in and hide on the far distant perimeter of the base and were now breaking out. The clicking I was hearing was the sound of the bullets moving through the air over my head. Or so I was told. Anyway, I also recall being quite pleased with myself that I managed not to get my dress dirty. Sometimes you have bizarre priorities at such moments.

I was later and often accused of having developed the "Intoxication with Cordite Syndrome" that sometimes infects the foolish in wartime. But if you truly believe you are not going to die, combat can be an exhilarating experience. Vann obviously felt that way too, right up until the moment he died. But I had thought it through, again logically, about those odds I relied on: a rare non-combatant female being killed in a random action in Vietnam? Even after all the possibilities in the fighting of Tet, I was still there, wasn't I? Proof enough for me! After the initial fear of that first night of Tet I was never seriously afraid again. Everything that followed, with a few variations, became just same old same old: bunkers, ditches, crash and bang, adrenalin kick-in, good luck holding.

Things began to quiet down after that as life and work took on a certain and more predictable routine. The Tet Offensive, as it came to be called, was later declared to be the turning point of the Vietnam War. Whether we won that battle or lost it was a matter of debate for years afterward – and to this day. This is a personal narrative of what I saw and did, so I will let the readers turn to the hundreds of books on the subject and come to their own conclusions. As for me, win or lose, I would not have missed it for the world.

Sally and I continued to meet occasionally and to date our pilots, but she eventually became involved with some Saigon warrior. I would occasionally join her at some event, at Saigon's Cercle Sportif, a colonial bastion full of Frenchified persons, or in one of the posh dining establishments that still abounded. I always felt slightly uncomfortable, indeed guilty, in those little islands of luxury (with a strong whiff of black marketeering) in the midst of war, privation and misery. I just wanted to hurry back to my boss and my buddies and the less comfortable but "real" life back in the field.

Sometimes when I think back on that whole wild Tet scene, I wonder if it all really happened to me, or could I have just imagined it? But decades later, I read a book by Don Oberdorfer called simply *Tet*. In, it was a bit about the Bien Hoa air base and a map that showed the control tower and the runways, and I could even pick out our bunker's general location on it – all right there and just where I remembered it. And although the details have mostly faded, I can recall certain aspects of that night as if it were only yesterday: the shock waves after the blasts, the eardrum-bursting din, the screams, the curses, the fear, the smell of cordite. All of it.

Yes, I was there.

5

THE NIGHT THE AMMO DUMP BLEW UP

GRADUALLY THE mortaring became less frequent, first every other night or so, then once a week. Our social activities thus began to return to their "pre-war" patterns of parties, bridge, poker, swimming, with the only difference being that we had a tendency to stay near home rather than going far afield and that we obeyed the curfew regulations with more enthusiasm – one drive through empty streets with a huge tank sitting right in the midst of the square and heavily-armed ARVN lurking in the darkness was enough to convince us that we were better off at home.

Most parties at the Franzblau started when the Ranch Hands completed their missions on Saturday and we had finally gotten away from the office. We would all gather in someone's apartment and start drinking and talking; the guys would gradually unwind and become more relaxed (and voluble). If there was no amah available and the numbers were small, then the gals would go into the kitchen and whip up some very casual meal, served with great abandon and lack of coordination. Since there were seldom enough chairs to go around, we mostly ate sitting around on the floor. The amahs would be back on Monday, so we could just leave the whole mess for them to clean up.

One particular Saturday night some days after Tet still stands out in my memory – and has since gone down in the annals of

Tet '68 history as "The Night the Ammo Dump Blew Up". Our guards on the roof never saw much worth firing at, but at the big Long Binh base a few miles away some guards must have been less alert to infiltrators than ours were.

After a busy day we had finished dinner and were lounging around chatting and drinking in an apartment on the top floor front of the building when someone happened to look out the window toward the army base at Long Binh and noticed an interesting red glow on the horizon. We all trooped out onto the balcony to see it, somewhat fuzzily offering our versions of what it might be. While we stood there enraptured by the sight, the red became redder and little white shoots began coming out at its edges, all gradually merging into a real pyrotechnic display. By then, we had cleverly deduced that the ammo dump must be on fire. Our interest was now riveted on that distant skyline and soon our attention was rewarded by a gigantic fireball that must have been about a quarter mile from edge to edge. We all gasped and someone said "My God, nukes!"

We stood there slack-jawed trying to take in what we were seeing – it looked exactly like the mushroom cloud in the photos of the atom bomb tests. We gazed, pop-eyed, while the whole horizon lit up like a gigantic Fourth of July fireworks display, only far, far bigger. Then it occurred to me that there had been no sound at all and I was about to comment on this when we were all almost blown over by a tremendous roar and wave of air. We wheeled in a panic and – as one – tried to get off the balcony through its single door, dropping drinks and trampling over each other in our haste to get away from whatever might come next (smoke, ashes, shards?).

We tumbled willy-nilly into the living room. Pictures were skewed on the walls and lamps had been tipped over, perhaps by us in our return flight. We flopped down on the floor and lay there stunned. A few of us inched over to lie behind our 300+ pound comrade "Tiny" (like African hunters shooting from behind an elephant). We realized what we had just seen was the Long Binh ammo dump blowing up.

The pyrotechnic display went on for hours. We probably lost five years' worth of ammo in that particular disaster – and in a war that was destined to go on even longer than that. We began to laugh with relief and as our heartbeats returned to normal, the whole thing got hilarious, especially our collective "acts of bravery" – when a more blatant case of "Every Man for Himself" would have been hard to find. We lay there, all sprawled out, soaked in spilled drinks, giggling and guffawing.

At that moment, the door opened and our particularly obnoxious and officious "apartment warden" came stomping in, flashing his .45 and swaggering like a cowboy. In reality, he was the equally officious functionary dealing primarily with the petty housekeeping functions of our offices and compounds, a job that he felt gave him preponderant authority and importance. Needless to say, we did not share this assessment. He took one look at the tipsy tangle of male and female bodies before him and immediately became "The Commanding General", barking orders to "report to our quarters" (we were in our quarters, f'gawdsake!). He then harrumphed a little when he saw that we were not heeding his pronouncements with due respect and informed us that from now on we females must report to him the presence of any male visitors in the evening hours. The "Brooklyn Razzberry" one of the guys gave him must have insulted him – as intended – and he wheeled and stalked out, revolver still in hand. It was all we could do to keep from laughing.

Considerably subdued now, both by the massive explosion and the unexpected and unwelcome appearance of our would-be commander, we decided all the life had gone out of the party anyway, so we dispersed to our various apartments; it was now well past curfew (as sleep-overs were by then the norm).

The next night, we gals began to rehash the whole thing and the more we discussed it, the madder we got. Who the hell did he think he was anyway, to give us orders like that? We agreed on a stinging memo to him and started working on our individual contributions to it. By the end of the week, and after much deliberation and redrafting, we came up with this memo to the officious Admin Officer.

FROM THE FEMALES AT THE FRANZBLAU

1. This is to request clarification of your oral directive of Saturday, 17 February 1968, ordering the female American occupants of the Franzblau Apartments to inform you of any overnight military-type male visitors they might have.
2. In our opinion this directive was extremely ill-conceived. We hope it was motivated by the desire to identify all additional manpower that might be available for defense purposes in an emergency. If so, it should have been clearly stated and directed to all occupants of the apartments regardless of sex inasmuch as male occupants also entertain male visitors here. We assume, and probably correctly, that this surveillance applies only to the apartments of the American "legal" female occupants of the Franzblau, and not to the numerous indigenous females to be found in other locations in the compound. Since it was only addressed to us, it represents rank discrimination.
3. In the event that our interpretation is incorrect and your statement, for some reason unknown to us, is in fact intended to apply only to the American female occupants of the Franzblau, we herewith submit the attached forms (a two-week supply) that are self-explanatory, for your convenience.
4. We would appreciate being informed of the exact time at which

the bed checks may be expected so as to avoid embarrassment to any visitors or the inconvenience of having to answer the door after having retired for the night. Inasmuch as working and sleeping hours are somewhat irregular at this time due to forces beyond our control, there exists the possibility of the bed check coming at an inconvenient time. To avoid undue disturbance we request GSO to furnish us with "Do Not Disturb" signs, and we would appreciate it if you would honor these.

5. You realize, of course, with the security situation being as tenuous and changeable as it is, unpremeditated overnight visits may occur at any time. Would you prefer to be informed of such visitations as they occur (sometimes quite late at night) or would an "after action" report suffice?

6. To simplify matters, you may want to consider the establishment of an Operations Center (with an adequate communications network) to which we could report the arrival and departure of our male visitors, together with their intentions (if known) – and ours – to establish a record for your subsequent perusal.

7. For further refinements, we refer you to George Orwell's book "1984".

To this, we appended a draft checklist entitled: "Female Occupants Daily Bed Check" with appropriate columns for findings, comparative scores, etc. Chortling happily at our cleverness, we had it all typed up and delivered to our victim, with ancillary copies to his boss, Vann, who we knew would get a big kick out of it. We also sent copies to all the American female occupants of the Franzblau, to show them we were looking out for their interests.

We later learned that Vann was so amused by the whole

thing that he read portions of the memo to visitors. I must admit that our (now badly mocked) addressee took the rebuff in good grace – or at least had the sense to pretend he did – although privately he would probably have liked to shoot us all. Our friends in the Ranch were of course delighted with the publication and posted it on their bulletin board, no doubt with appropriate lewd comments. Needless to say, we had no more trouble regarding late night visits by male officers to Franzblau's females.

There is still one more tale of yet another night that is universally remembered by all Tet survivors lucky enough to be watching on television the film "Love is A Many Splendored Thing". Perhaps because it was about Asia and unrequited love, that particular movie was heavily viewed on that particular night, at least if subsequent recountings of this story are true. Right at the point where Jennifer Jones is coming over the hill and sees the ghost of her beloved American doctor, a really heavy rocket attack commenced and all threw themselves onto the floor and crawled to their self-prepared shelters. By the time the rocketing ended and they emerged, the movie was over and the Ten O' Clock News was telling them it was a quiet night in the Republic of Vietnam – a statement that was probably met with catcalls. But to this day, whenever you talk to anyone who was in the Saigon area that night and you start out by saying, "Remember the night that 'Love is a…' – and they immediately chime in:

"Yeah, remember when she was coming over the hill and…"

and then you both chime in together: "…all those rockets started coming in!"

That means you are part of the special little band of brothers who were in that place at that time and who will never again be able to see an advertisement for "Love is a Many Splendored Thing" (or "Love is a Many Splendored Egg Roll" as we liked to call it) without thinking back on that noisy night.

THE NIGHT THE AMMO DUMP BLEW UP

6

BACK TO "NORMAL"

LIFE IN BIEN HOA rapidly returned to a (revised) state of "normal". Our work hours now extended from 8:00am until 8:00pm as a whole spate of new reporting requirements to our Situation Reports - or Sit Reps - arose. Since everyone was working the same hours or longer, at first we didn't notice the added load. In fact, we hesitated to leave the office lest we miss some of the latest news coming in from the provinces. Getting up in the morning was now no problem; every morning about dawn a multitude of choppers took off from the field directly behind the Franzblau - and barely cleared our rooftop from the sound of it. This never failed to bring us out of beds with a start, and once awake, the din of ordinary Vietnamese street life finished the job.

The nights, too, began to fall into a pattern. The Air Force was restricted to the base - a restriction that was only lifted many months later - which meant that my only chance to see Bob was to go to the base for dinner. We would meet at the O Club for a drink, then have dinner there - a much easier process now that the Vietnamese waitresses were no longer allowed on the base and the Club had gone to cafeteria style.

The Ranch was doing the cursed "trash-hauling" (moving supplies around the countryside, often to small outposts with short landing strips) and both Happy Hour and dinner usually evolved into a long string of gripes revolving around the day's foul-ups. Trash hauling definitely represented the lowest form of pilot life as far as the Ranch Hands were concerned. In fact, after the first few days of elation due to the previous overactive adrenalin rushes, they were all finding the new and daily routine both boring and wearing.

We were still having mortar attacks – or false alarms – almost every night. If they didn't hit Bien Hoa, then they were sure to try for Long Binh and the III Corps military headquarters there. The Air Force was required to take to the bunkers in all alerts rather than wait to see if it was real and in the near vicinity. In the early days at the Franzblau we just rolled out of our beds and crawled into the kitchen, our own personal mortar shelter by virtue of its having no outside windows. For the Ranch Hands this interruption of much-needed sleep, especially since trash hauling usually began about 4:00am, also had a tendency to make the Ranch Hands slightly peevish and the prevailing mood was of low-level irritability, relieved usually by generous lashings of alcohol.

After a drink or two we would eat our dinners at one of the smaller tables and leave the rest of the Ranch Hands to complain about their new schedule, the brass, and the war in general. We would discuss the risks of going AWOL (meaning off-base), how our day had gone, what the night promised (often gleaned from our five o'clock briefings) and what we intended to do about it – mostly nothing except to call each other after the night's attacks were over to be sure we were both OK. I would then walk with Bob back to his hooch where we would sit on some sandbags and watch the preparations for the nightly mortar attacks: the usual re-stacking of sandbags and critical examination of secondary defense positions. Men were again dragging their mattresses into bunkers (now allowed) – where some had slept all night every night since the beginning of the Tet offensive.

Sitting there in the darkness of our little corner, we were virtually alone and unseen, lights and voices muted, surrounded by a bustle of activity but totally ignored, which suited us just fine. It gave us a deceptively peaceful setting, with the warm tropical night occasionally illuminated by a flare. It was sometimes quite still and on other nights noisy with the sounds of war: small arms fire in the distance, the brrrrrpppppp of Gatling guns, sometimes muffled explosions.

We finally kissed each other a reluctant goodnight and I started the drive back along the perimeter road, my mind totally absorbed in thoughts: of Bob, of work and whatever else people think of when they drive along darkened roads alone. Suddenly there was a series of white plumes which seemed to erupt from the earth a way off to the left of the road and I thought I heard a couple of thuds over the sound of my radio blaring away. But I was now in a hurry to get home so I just kept on driving. That is, until I came upon a jeep in the middle of the road with men piling out of it and hurling themselves into the ditch at the side of the road. They saw me and motioned frantically.

I stopped and rolled down the window to hear what they were saying. The gist of it was "Get down, get down, we're being mortared!" A few more thuds and flashes convinced me they just might be right and so I got out of the car and skittered over to a portion of the ditch illuminated by headlights. Even if did not have my white dress on this time, I still didn't plan to leap into some filth if it was not absolutely necessary.

By now the men, with that Protect-American-Womanhood gleam in their eyes, were more emphatic in their directions, and I gingerly crouched in a cruddy, but fortunately non-cesspooly ditch, feeling both silly and exposed. A few more thuds of diminishing intensity and then dead silence. I wondered idly if this signaled the beginning of a ground attack since it was much earlier than the usual nightly barrage. The young soldier lying a few feet away from me must have had the same idea: his eyes were big as saucers as he stared out toward the thin line of concertina wire that separated us from the perimeter fields. The nearest guard post was several hundred yards away and the guards on duty were undoubtedly sharing our anxieties.

As the night became still again, we gradually relaxed and the young soldier nearby in my ditch had one of those I'm-from-Texas-where-are-you-from conversations with me, complete with all the social amenities. I had to laugh to myself at the picture we presented: two people crouched down in a ditch having a most proper and interesting cocktail-party conversation – another of the many incongruities of Vietnam. We finally decided it was all over, exchanged pleasantries and went our separate ways.

I could hardly wait to get home to call Bob and say "Guess what just happened to me!" He proved, however, somewhat less than amused by the whole thing and berated himself because he had not driven to the front gate with me and thus had left me exposed to danger all by myself. I wisely kept my mouth shut and did not tell him that actually I had been in little real danger – and had a very nice conversation to boot.

The weeks went by, punctuated by little flurries of enemy activity and longer periods of waiting for new assaults. Gradually the pieces fell into place and we learned how the enemy had managed to infiltrate in such strength as to partially overrun the airfield and the town. The "friendly" little Catholic village of Ho Nai, four miles down the road had for several weeks before Tet harbored over a hundred VC and NVA troops without any of our (paid) informers revealing this fact to us. Their threats of reprisal to the village chief and the priest, both highly respected and beloved men, had done the trick – and how could you blame them?

Many of the enemy troops had hidden in the little church, now a pock-marked ruin from the fighting. I suspected the destruction of the church would be remembered long after the presence of the VC was forgotten. When I thought of all the times I had driven through Ho Nai in the past month, with those impassive faces staring at me from alongside the road, I marveled anew that we were ever able to ferret out the enemy in this conflicted country or that we could ever positively identify a VC even when we caught a suspect. Just another of the frustrations of fighting a land war in a country about which we really knew so little.

7

A TRIP TO THE COMMISSARY

AS OUR FOOD supplies became depleted, several of us we decided we would have to make a commissary run to Saigon. We dreaded that even in more peaceful days because it was always so time-consuming and sweat-producing. We started out at nine on a Saturday morning with the driver assigned for the run in our big American station wagon. The sky was cloudless and already the temperature was in the upper nineties. As we were in the dry season, fine dust covered all the highways and blew through the open windows onto us, churned up by each passing vehicle. The trip to the "superhighway" was slow and tortuous, as it was still market time in the few small villages we went through, with their narrow streets lined with pushcarts and squatting farmers' wives with their wares spread out on shelter halves. People spilled out into the main road, most often looking neither left nor right as they moved from one side to the other in the sublime belief that Buddha would protect them. The driver used the brakes and the horn alternately, with emphasis on the latter.

We finally reached the main highway and found it jammed with the usual morning traffic plus a convoy of trucks and APC's (armored personnel carriers) proceeding from Long Binh to Saigon loaded with men and gear. They waved and hollered and gave us the "V" sign as we maneuvered in and out of the long column. The highway was four lanes with an extra strip on each side to allow vehicles to pull off the road when disabled – a concept which unfortunately never completely caught on in Vietnam.

I remember once coming up over the prow of a hill and finding my lane blocked by a large truck with the hood gaping open. Traffic was swerving around it but unmoved by it all was the driver, who had stretched his hammock underneath the underpinnings of the high truck bed and lay there swinging back and forth gently with a serene smile on his face as traffic somehow slowly maneuvered around him. Drivers of disabled vehicles – and almost every second Vietnamese vehicle is disabled at one time or another – mostly work on their problems right there on the busy highway, with tools clustered around their feet and cars whizzing by inches from their bodies. The fact that most of them seemed to survive was a tribute to some unspoken code of the road.

The largest bridge between Bien Hoa and Saigon had reputedly been blown up by sappers but at least one lane was supposed to have been repaired and opened to traffic. However, about five miles this side of the bridge, the traffic was halted and we could see it stretching in an unmoving column far in front of us. Most of the drivers had shut off their engines and were squatting beside the road, smoking and chatting. Toward us in the other lane came a thin stream of slow-moving vehicles. Heading in both directions, snaking in and out of the parked and moving vehicles, were the ubiquitous motorbikes emitting gaseous fumes and clouds of blue smoke, to say nothing of noise.

They would proceed at their own pace until they too were jammed up against an immovable barrier, where they would gun their motors and fret and circle and maneuver for position so as to be the first to shoot through when it opened. We sat in the sweltering heat for maybe twenty minutes and finally there was a buzz of anticipation and activity and the line in front of us suddenly began to lurch forward, a few feet at a time, with everyone jockeying for position, including mopeds inserting themselves in any gap between autos. You had to keep the bumper of your car almost on the bumper of the car in front of you lest some sort of motorized vehicle stick its snout in between and you became one car farther back in the line.

Proceeding in this competitive fashion amidst much blowing of horns and billows of raw exhaust fumes, we finally inched up to the bridge, only to be cut off about five cars from our goal in order to let the oncoming traffic once again proceed. Since at least five cars had shoved their way in front of us in our journey at this point, it only increased our frustration. From the elevated bridge ramp, we had an excellent view of the damage: one whole span of the bridge was dropped about four feet and hanging by some steel cables. Luckily this only happened in two lanes, but it gave me some doubts about the remaining two lanes that we, along the many overloaded trucks, were traveling on.

The small guard house was shot up and there were huge holes blown in the larger concrete building that used to house the guards. All of the remaining walls were pockmarked with bullet holes. Armed guards stood all along the bridge watching the creeping traffic with bored expressions, their weapons pointed toward the sky and braced on their hips with the ever-ready finger resting on the trigger. Since they always kept a round chambered, this accounted for the frequency of the shots one heard around a guard posts night and day. (It's a miracle they didn't shoot each other.)

We finally cleared the bridge in a burst of speed as we came out of the narrow pass like cattle out of a chute and were relieved to suddenly be moving at more than twenty miles an hour. Motorbikes passed us indiscriminately to the left and right, often so close they brushed against the side of the car. As we moved into the built-up suburbs, I noted that certain city blocks bore the scars of war while others seemed relatively untouched. One square block was virtually leveled but was already being rebuilt; some buildings were mere concrete shells with gaping windows and doors and rebuilding would involve recreating the interior of the structure. In fact, despite the widespread photos of the devastation of the Cho Lon area featured prominently in the American newspapers, within months of the Tet Offensive, it was hard to discern any damage at all; only an occasional pock-marked wall indicated the fierce fighting that had leveled a great swath of the area such a short a time ago.

This was hard to explain to my American friends, especially the older generation familiar with pictures of the damage in Berlin and other major German cities during the war. I suppose all ruins look alike to a layman, but I was constantly startled to be asked, "Is there anything left standing in Saigon?" People were very skeptical of my explanation that there may be things not standing, but in most parts of the city, war damage was not in evidence despite the street fighting that had raged there during the first few days of Tet.

The American Embassy had not been so lucky as it was not only shot up, but the VC had managed to enter its ground floor, even as the Americans trapped on the floors above were sending out distress calls. They were finally relieved by American troops and with only a few casualties. The photos in the American newspapers, however, had horrified the general public and the Viet Cong's success against this symbol of American strength was a real 'black eye' to the prestige of the Americans – in a war that they we claimed to be winning.

We wound our way into Cho Lon to the compound where the commissary was located. Parking places were as usual at a premium and our driver had to double park and wait until a place opened up. The second we alighted, we were surrounded by a mob of children, ages roughly five to ten, who jostling us begging for chewing gum or cigarettes or giving us the old "you buy for me" plea. We held our purses high over our heads and waded on through, telling them in Vietnamese to go play, trot along etc, which they took with good grace and finally wandered off. We knew with certainty, however, that they would be there waiting for us as we emerged with our loaded shopping carts. If we got 95% of our purchases back to the car we would be lucky, since the groceries were pushed in carts for us by Vietnamese porters and thus were at child-level as they moved along.

During the rush hours, admission had to be controlled to prevent over-crowding. About twenty people stood patiently in the skimpy shade by the commissary wall. Periodically the door would open and two or three would be admitted. Admissions, it turned out, were also regulated by the number of carts available; only if you were willing to try to carry everything in your arms could you, grudgingly, be allowed to buck the line. Since we needed many weeks' worth of all-American dinner fixings, for us the shortcut was not an option.

We finally got in, scanned the aisles and loaded our carts. Then another long wait as the check-out line inched forward. Everyone's cart was overflowing with groceries and some lucky (or unlucky, depending on your point of view) people had two carts completely loaded to the gunwales. The checker moved with the grace and speed of a classical dancer and everything moved at a leisurely pace, but eventually she completed our computations. We did not complain since the cash register was at least functioning, unlike some of them down the line. We occasionally rolled our eyes heavenward but there was obviously no help from there – at least not in this Buddhist land.

The Vietnamese loader at the end of the counter pounced with gusto on the pile of groceries. We gently corrected his inclination to put the bread and tomatoes on the bottom and the canned goods on top. We rescued the frozen foods and put them in the Styrofoam chest we had brought with us. My humble purchases alone completely filled one flat-bottom cart, somewhat like the ones used to tote luggage in old railroad stations. I walked along beside it as we proceeded to the parking lot outside the gate.

The children spotted us and leaped into action, circling and darting around us. I fended them off with my Vietnamese version of "go away", *di di mau*. The driver saw us coming and joined us in the fray, neatly turning the tide. We loaded our things in the back of the station wagon where the temperature was about 100 degrees. I gave the bearer a generous tip and, to make assurance doubly sure, gave the driver "lunch" money so that we could go back into the compound and have some lunch while he guarded the booty.

The snack bar emitted the all-American odor of stale French fries and cigarette smoke. It too was hot and crowded but promised us on large signs a glacial Coke in a frosted glass portrayed next to a mouth-watering hotdog on a roll. Alas, when we got to the head of the line we found the ice machine had long ago given up, and they no longer had hot dogs. But they managed to rustle up something on bread for sandwiches and tepid glasses of limeade; as it was at least not at body temperature we were slightly refreshed.

We agreed that the secret to happiness is to think small and not wish for too much. My mind wandered back to pictures of colonials sitting on verandahs while white-robed servants brought them long drinks. I made a mental vow that I would foreswear all these American conveniences to which I was enslaved and start living the good "colonial" life forthwith, unburdened by commissary and PX runs. I would go native with a vengeance.

Yeah, sure...

We collected our wits and emerged into the steamy heat. Even the street urchins had retreated under shade and were not there to harass us. Our driver was sprawled out on the back seat of the station wagon, his bare feet sticking out the window, a wet towel over his eyes. He opened the door, we sank back on our seats and began the long trip home. Conversation consisted of an occasional grunt, or shriek when a crash appeared imminent. Between these exertions we slumped, eyes half closed against the dust, jostling against each other with the sway of the car.

We followed a tri-Lambretta trucklet, its back completely filled with green bananas on which lay two peasant women, their heads wrapped in what appeared to be dishcloths, soundly sleeping with their mouths open and arms and legs sprawled out like disjointed dolls. We envied them for their adaptability. Then there was a Citroen sedan which had been overrun by an ARVN truck until it now stood about three feet high, accordion pleated in front. It seems unlikely that any of its occupants could have survived. We waited our allotted time at the bridge, only this time it was faster because the convoy that had priority over the civilian traffic had long ago moved on. When we arrived back in our cool and calm apartments, our amahs were waiting for us. We simply turned everything over to them and headed for the showers and a long nap, to be followed by a delicious dinner.

Colonialism again reigns.

8

FROM WAR TO PEACE

ONE NIGHT BOB and I were invited to a party given by the local "spooks" (members of an intelligence community). They always seemed to live down dark alleys, thinking it gave them a low profile, I assume (although of course all the Vietnamese knew who they were and exactly where they lived.) Trying to remember the instructions we had been given to find the right alleyway, Bob and I wandered down Bien Hoa's darkened back streets somewhere near the river. In the dim distance, we saw a big shadowy object that looked like a tank and behind it some sort of a pillbox. We had just begun to ventilate our apprehensions about the whole setup when we must have trod on a trip wire and two flares suddenly shot up into the air and burst above us, scaring us out of our wits.

After a moment, we realized what must have happened and glanced around us. There in front of us was indeed a compound, not the one we sought but an ARVN one. We fancied we saw beady eyes peering out through the gun slots, but we did not stay around to find out what sort of a viper's nest we had stumbled onto. As one, we silently wheeled around and, mustering as much dignity as we could under the circumstances, managed to walk, not run, back down the alley. Only after we were around a corner and completely out of firing range did our hearts slow down enough that I could gasp, "My God, what was that!?"

We never found that night's party; we were so rattled by our experience that we returned home and had a stiff drink. We also chose never to return to that sector again by daylight or dark – and we never did find out if that was some contractor's private army, a spook outfit or what. The experience only reinforced my private theory that we were often in more danger from the Friendlies than from the enemy.

Often when I would work late at night – that's when much of the office work got done after the bosses' long day in the field – I would nip home for dinner and then drive in my little VW back to the headquarters. When we finally finished up, it would be long after curfew and the streets would be deserted except for the RF/PF (Regional Forces/Provincial Forces – or Ruff-Puffs to us), and mostly teenagers – and occasionally the PSDF (People's Self-Defense Force), the latter looking a bit older. They all carried loaded carbines which they handled with great abandon, sometime filling the night air with loud bursts of gunfire, often a clip at a time.

I would turn on the overhead light in my car as I drove very slowly through the darkened town. At the main square by the water tank, there was always a large American tank manned by ARVN soldiers clustered around it. We regarded each other warily and I sometimes gave a little wave as I went by; they stared impassively, except for the occasional hawk and spit. There was always so much random gunfire everywhere that when I got back to the Franzblau, I would call the office and tell them I had arrived home.

Since Vann apparently knew no fear himself (amply documented) he did not expect anyone else to have any either. More than a few bright and brave young lads died trying to live up to Vann's expectations. But he felt very strongly his responsibility for their deaths and it preyed on his mind at times, especially when he had to write the bereavement letters to the grieving parents. Although they were formulaic, he always added personal (and moving) comments and I would often weep as we typed them. We thought of that as his Achilles Heel. With all of his staff, his brief was simple and straightforward: You know the country and the situation. Use your heads. Go anywhere you want to go and if you get killed, I'll say you were on official business to cover for you. So we all happily and freely operated under that rubric – sometimes to the point of foolhardy folly.

Our most frequent visitor was General Fred Weyand, who had previously commanded the II Field Force in the province to our north and now had been moved down to III Corps. Weyand was one of the very few generals in Vietnam who did not go to West Point but came up through the ranks, which made him a GI's General. He was a very warm and likeable guy, hence one of our favorites. He and Vann were straight-talkers and very outspoken and you could see why they had become friends.

In looking up the date of Weyand's death (in 2010 at age ninety-three), I found his prophetic quote from an informal setting in Saigon in 1967 (!). Speaking of General Westmoreland, he said: "Westy just doesn't get it. The war is unwinnable. We've reached a stalemate, and we should find a dignified way out."

And that before the Tet offensive and eight years before the end. It was also Weyand, then commander of US forces in the Saigon-Bien Hoa area, whose troops stopped the attackers during Tet, probably saving us all from further harm. He did it from his nearby HQ in the Long Binh Army Base, which was in sight of the air base, rather than from the safer and far more distant Saigon. He was such a great guy and so popular with all of us.

Our office's military contingent at that time consisted of a Chief Warrant Officer who was the pilot for Vann's chopper (al-

though Vann mostly flew it himself), and also often served as
our general factotum and "horse-holder", plus two EMs who
did everything else. Newly attached to us was also a young and
green Lieutenant whose assignment one day was to go to the
chopper pad about 500 yards up the road and meet the General
who wanted to consult with Vann before making a visual sweep
of the area, lead him to the waiting jeep, and see that he was ac-
companied to our office.

We reminded the Lieutenant repeatedly of the General's ETA
but he dawdled and finally got out the door only about two minutes before it. As he and his driver were driving along, they spotted Weyand and his aide striding down the dusty road toward
them. The Lieutenant, envisioning his silver bars fluttering away
into the sunset, leaped from the jeep, saluted smartly, and said,
"General, sir, would you like a ride, sir?"

Weyand smiled and said that he preferred to walk, so he and
the Lieutenant strode down the road together, the jeep slowly
following along behind them. We saw them coming through the
parking lot and, after one look at the procession, divined immediately what had happened. Not a word was ever said about the
screw-up, but afterwards the Lieutenant consistently arrived at
the chopper pad at least half an hour before the arrival of the
VIPs – and for early morning arrivals we had to dissuade him
from sleeping there overnight in his jeep.

One Saturday night I, Frenchy and two new (probably CIA)
gals recently assigned somewhere in Bien Hoa were invited to
the Special Forces compound at the far end of the base. The ri-
valry between the hard-drinking, womanizing pilots and their
testosterone-filled rivals was palpable from the very first. The clientele was Americans of all ranks and the cost of drinks was only
about fifty cents equivalent in Vietnamese currency. (Surprisingly there was seldom any friction between the flyboy officers and

their own EMs; the latter were often the aircraft mechanics on whom any flight depended and the pilots were acutely aware of their importance.)

As we walked into that gigantic room that night, four Round Eyes and the only ones in the room, every eye was on us. As long as I had Bob behind me, I was always able to manage a serene entry. It was only when one of us gals had to go to the ladies' room that I got nervous. The trip there was no problem, but often our audience would wait for us to exit and then it was to wild cheers, whistles and ribaldry (and occasionally even a fanfare by the band) as we slunk back to our table where our dates sometimes gave us a standing ovation. It was all a great inducement to bladder control.

I don't want to give the erroneous impression that we females were always the picture of sobriety. Among us, the drinking patterns ranged from hollow legs to those – and I am one, alas – who can get drunk just smelling a beer bottle cap. I certainly must have been the cheapest date in town at their Happy Hour prices, a fact which probably pleased Bob no end.

One of the favorite Ranch Hand tricks was to demand that we give a toast, hoist one of us up onto the table (especially if you were wearing a mini-skirt) and then go silent to await your presentation. The only catch was that the moment you started to speak they immediately drowned you out with cheers and howls. I was, however, soon on to their game so instead of even trying to start a speech I would shout "To the Ranch" and raise my glass. They had to respond appropriately, so they soon gave up on me and searched for other targets.

The usual Vietnamese band played all through the long evenings – a remarkable feat when you consider that they apparently knew only about six songs. (Until the day I die, I will always be able to hear in my head their "Yellow River" as rendered by the local vocalist as "Yerrow Liver.")

Later in the night when fistfights were about to break out, the bar manager lowered the lights and the combo broke into a sensuous wail. Out strolled a Vietnamese stripper wearing a spangly dress, high-heeled shoes and sporting an "enhanced" set of boobs. That the young lady was remarkably well-endowed really did not matter all that much, as in this setting any bare body guaranteed a howling success. The guys were in for a real treat – the famous local "beaver" show. The only thing raunchier than a beaver show is a "split-beaver" show (don't ask) – and unfortunately this one fell into that category.

Suffice it to say the audience loved it all, and since the room was now darkened – for which we were grateful – our distaff presence was soon forgotten. We gals exited shortly after the show (the curfew was still on) and learned later that it all went to hell in a handbasket after the show with the usual bar fights and drunken brawling.

Our pilots' later comments: "Dumb grunts – always looking for a fight."

9

AN AMERICAN INTERLUDE

POST-TET LIFE, even in wartime Vietnam, became a little routine and boring. And when I get bored I get restless. I decided that maybe it was time to get back to "real life", the United States of America.

Even before I left, Bob had already rotated back to the USA. We bade farewell to each other in Bien Hoa, knowing that we would never see each other again.

Back home I mused over whether I would want to go back to my old teaching job but decided that, after Vietnam service, I really did not want to return to that quaint small town and pick up where I had left off. When I asked to transfer back to the US, the Saigon Personnel Officer told me that all I had to do was say I was afraid of staying on in Vietnam and I could have my way paid home. It was tempting, but I was not afraid and I simply could not say that I was in order to save a few thousand dollars. As it turned out, telling the truth was the wisest measure. In 1969, I paid my way home on the *U.S.S. President Cleveland* visited friends in California and then drove back to Virginia. That drive across the vast, fertile and peaceful countryside of Middle America really made me appreciate anew what a wonderful country it was and what a privileged life we lead.

While I debated what to do next, I decided to become a ski bum in Aspen. I bought a condo and got a part-time job in a downtown real estate office. I filled my free time with skiing. I discovered what I should have known: that when you can ski all the time, it is not half as much of a treat as when it can only be done on precious few weekends or week-long skiing vacations. So I went back east and got a job at the Institute for International Living in Vermont. My next discovery was that, as a Southerner, I didn't belong in the frozen north, or in fact anywhere north of the Mason-Dixon Line.

I was obviously floundering. I was really missing Vietnam. I missed my comrades in arms, the challenges, the beautiful countryside and its gentle people who deserved so much more than they were getting. I especially missed the sense of purpose that pervaded all our work, all our efforts. I went back down to Virginia, called the USAID Personnel Office, and asked if there was any possibility for me to be sent back to Vietnam. This was probably an unusual question, as most of the requests were probably from people asking to come home from, not to go back to, Vietnam.

The Personnel Officer looked at my record, saw that I had left Vietnam "for personal reasons" and at my own expense, and may have thought I'd had a family emergency or some such; she did not ask and I did not have to explain my change of heart. Thanks to having told the truth upon my departure, in less than a year I was back in Vietnam. Proving that Virtue is indeed (sometimes) rewarded.

Upon my return in 1969 I found that Vann had taken over the DEPCORDS job in IV Corps and he and Colonel Wilson were now down in the Delta. Vann agreed to take me back on board, knowing that I was a solid staffer who could be counted on to stay the course – my recent defection notwithstanding – and get the job done. And he always was a push-over to requests from females. I was back in. Again, just lucky.

10

VANN IN THE DELTA – A LAST GOODBYE

THE WAR WAS still going on in the provinces of the Delta but there had been no recent attacks in Can Tho, the provincial capital and corps headquarters for the Vietnamese military. I decided to drive down with a colleague also going that way. It was a long and interesting drive. The main highway southward, certainly not built to support the current traffic load, was filled with every conceivable form of transport from oxcarts to bicycles to overloaded buses with swaying loads on top and people hanging on and jumping off the sides. The war appeared to have settled down for a long slog and this area was now peaceful so peasants were heading to markets, families going from Saigon back home to the countryside, life resuming its routine workaday activities. The drive also involved a ferry crossing and waiting patiently in long lines – not something the Vietnamese are noted for – and the trip offered a panoply of Vietnamese life on the move in this verdant countryside. Although I later drove the Can Tho to Saigon road relatively seldom – we always seemed to be in a hurry to get somewhere – it was certainly never a boring trip.

Our usual mode of transportation between Saigon and most places was by plane on the Air America (run by the CIA) daily shuttles, typically in a Caribou. It was a great way to see the countryside since the loading bay in the back remained open during the flights. We sat in bucket seats along the side with cargo usually filling the space in the middle. As we flew fairly low there was no need for cabin pressurization and it was great fun to stand at the back and look down over the lush green of the delta as it unrolled below us.

Arriving in Can Tho, I was back at work for the same bosses in the same office, and again with Frenchy, only now in a more distant (at least from Saigon) location. I was soon ensconced in my new quarters and it was as if I had never left Vietnam. Can Tho lay about a hundred miles south of Saigon on a tributary of the Mekong River. For Vann, this was familiar territory; he had been in the Delta in 1963 at a seminal moment in his military life there, a debacle called the Battle of Ap Bac. But that is another story and not mine.

The CORDS housing compound was called Palm Springs and it actually had palm trees and – what a luxury – a swimming pool. (In 2009, it had all disappeared without trace.) During my tour there would be numerous parties around the pool, including the post's biggest annual event, the Independence Day barbeque – that I soon learned I was going to be in charge of organizing. Vann would also hold his formal awards ceremonies here – we were always getting "awards and decs" (decorations) and/or medals for something or other. One of my dachshunds would occasionally wander past the lectern while Vann was reading out the names of the recipients standing stiffly at attention. It never fazed Vann – he never sweated the small stuff – but I suspect it must have been a bit off-putting to those who took these things suitably seriously.

As we only worked until 1:00pm on most Saturdays, we often lolled around the pool in our bikinis with our dates before dressing to go out in the evening.

To jump forward several decades, I must share a funny Can

Tho/Shanghai story. My recent co-author Deke Erh, a Shanghainese from a conservative family, started creating books with me in 1991 when I was sixty years old. He expressed an interest in Vietnam, and I showed him my Vietnam War photos. As he leafed through them, he spotted one of me in a bikini sitting by the pool at Palm Springs. He paused, looked up at me, looked down again at the photo, then said in obvious astonishment: "That was you!?" He was genuinely shocked. I guess it never occurred to him that I had not always been old.

The Can Tho accommodations were a little less luxurious than in Bien Hoa; this time it was I who would be living in a hooch. These were a bit bigger than the Ranch ones, as here they had to accommodate four singles and a big square wooden hooch had been divided into four separate two-room "apartments". The front part of each had screened windows and held a tiny kitchen tucked into one end. There we ate the delicious food prepared by our Vietnamese amahs (mine stole me blind, but never mind). A sturdy, lockable door led into the main room that served us for everything else. All four apartments met at the center where four bathrooms were clustered around a plumbing core. It was a rather cozy arrangement, as you could be brushing your teeth or showering and clearly hear one of your neighbors doing the same – or something else. Needless to say, we all kept our radios on loud in our bathrooms. A built-in closet along one common wall provided a bit of sound-proofing, and our loud air-conditioners did the rest.

The best thing about tin-roofed hooches was that when it rained it started with a gentle drumming on the roof – that was the pleasant part – and then crescendo'd into a thunderous beating that made you feel like you were inside a snare drum. The start of the monsoon season was such a relief after the increasingly oppressive heat and humidity that preceded it that the local children ran out into the streets and splashed and danced, turning their little faces up to the sky to welcome the cooling rain. It was a refreshing and reinvigorating season in Vietnam.

I installed a water bed in the living/bedroom – water beds stay quite cool – and there was just enough room left over for a small sofa and a few chairs. Most visitors soon learned to ignore the bed right in the middle of the room, as I would later do in Shanghai in the homes of Chinese friends. Some visitors, however, like the GIs who took the University of Maryland class in German that I taught there, liked to try it out after the class, bouncing and swaying with its waves. They all loved it and whether it was solely responsible for the increase in the number of GIs wanting to study German in my "home room" class I cannot say.

Palm Springs was just one kilometer or so from our office so it was an easy commute; we could drive home for lunch, grab a quick bite to eat and then have a swim or a nap – both latter soon becoming addictive in the tropical heat. We still started work early and finished late but the Mekong Delta seemed much more peaceful, more "pacified", than the provinces in III Corps had been – but of course this was also a year later. At least, I do not recall a single rocket attack in Can Tho (although I might have slept through some aimed at more distant local targets).

There was both an Army and an Air Force base on the outskirts of Can Tho but not close enough to serve as mortar magnets for us in the city's center. I had occasion to visit both and I soon noted the difference between how the Army lived in contrast to the Air Force. The Army base was mostly asphalt and packed earth. It looked sort of raggedy with no attempt to smarten it up. Sagging sandbagged bunkers were scattered around the compound as I think they sometimes got the rocket attacks that we downtown did not.

On the Air Force base there was a flagpole in a little square near the entrance, with whitewashed rocks bordering it and flowers planted around it. (Maybe they even had a flag-lowering ceremony each night?) There were some bunkers, perhaps for the enlisted men but each officer's hooch had a crawl space cut into the outer wall beside the beds. When the alarm sounded, all they had to do was to roll out of bed, crawl through the wall opening, lie down on a mattress already in place there and go back to sleep. The officers had all chipped in to hire Vietnamese laborers to build sloping concrete revetments against the sides of their hooches, and to put thick concrete on the tops and then cut openings through the hooches' outer walls for the occupants to access these shelters. A practical, even ingenious, arrangement, it seemed to me.

We soon fell into the same work pattern as in Bien Hoa, Vann in one office and Colonel Wilson on the opposite side. Frenchy and I this time sharing an office that separated them. The area between her desk and mine served as a thoroughfare to offices behind us, occupied by EMs who did most of the routine administrative stuff that we were spared. The second floor had other officers, among them one of the two Saigon Embassy's provincial reporters who covered the Mekong Delta. One of our civilian officers, Lacy Wright did his own reports, but I would see him often when he entered and exited the building. Lacy was the congenial (and very witty) guy who was also the Political Advisor (POLAD) to Vann, and we later (and in Saigon) became friends.

When I consulted him seeking further info on Vann for this book, Lacy gave me an interesting piece of information I had never read before that I think illustrates how eager Vann was to get his message out to a wider world.

"When I left in September of 1970, Vann asked me to stay on but I had already been assigned to London. He then told me he would soon go to the US on home leave and asked if, once I got to London, I would persuade the Embassy there to request that he stop in London on his way back to Vietnam and brief the Ambassador and other staff on how the war was going. I did, and he came. He stayed with me in my apartment for three days, during which I got him dates with two young women who worked at the Embassy. The first was a proper girl from the American south; we double-dated and saw a London musical. The second was a British girl of about 21, who, the following day, asked me, 'Who was that man?' Vann departed at dawn from my place on the fourth day. It was the last time I would see him."

For Vann the Vietnam War was his crusade -- indeed an obsession -- and anything else was secondary. He would do anything and go anywhere to further his vision of how it could be won. And I think toward the end he still pursued a victory at any cost..I think we all knew all along that he would never ever give up, even until his last breath. And indeed that is the way it worked out…

The second building in our compound was also a three-storey concrete building with a roof strong enough to support Vann's chopper. This was a little Huey LOH (Light Observation Helicopter, pronounced loach); it looked like an egg with a tiny spinner on a tail. Fast and very maneuverable, it was just what Vann needed for swooping down to get a close look at things. It was unarmed (only Huey gunships had guns), but of course Vann himself always traveled well-armed, both in his chopper and in the white Ford that he drove as daringly as he flew – and almost as fast.

I remember Vann telling us, after returning from a drive through VC country, that he'd been ambushed as he slowed down at a checkpoint. At the first shot, he floored the Ford. He always drove with the front windows open and several hand grenades on the seat beside him, pins removed and levers held down only by tape. He ripped off the tape with his teeth and tossed a grenade out of each window as he roared past. He emerged untouched and with only a bullet hole in the Ford to confirm his tale. We never doubted him, trust me.

Vann had his own personal pilot, always a young CWO (Chief Warrant Officer), but he usually flew the chopper himself and had the pilot in the left seat. If the pilot was not lounging around in our office, as he did mostly on hot days, we had a set routine: When Vann was about two minutes from take-off one of us would ring a bell that sounded on the roof. We would then go outside to where the pilot could see us from above, twirl our fingers like a rotor blade and hold up the number of fingers that indicated the minutes until take-off. At the proper time the pilot would crank it up, Vann would dash out, run up the stairs, jump in and take off. He did not like to waste a moment of his time and his days stretched for so many hours that we could never figure out when he slept (only about three hours a night, it turned out).

When he was going out to some especially remote or hard-hit provincial outpost, he would often have someone go down to the market and buy a case of mangoes, bananas, or another of the tropical fruits that abounded in the Delta, and have them loaded aboard. Often the men in the smaller outposts did not dare to leave their fortified positions, or to let any unknown Vietnamese into the compound lest he be a VC infiltrator, restricting their diet to boring field rations. The Delta may have been more pacified than up north, but security was pretty patchy; some of the more remote areas were hardly pacified at all – and those were the places that Vann really liked to go.

He was a great morale builder – as well as career builder – and he really took good care of his men, but all his geese were swans. We all felt that he carried a lot of dead wood to greater heights through his influence; if you were a "Vann Man" you had it made. I remember sitting in a briefing where he was extolling the Vietnamese language fluency of one of his dim-bulb civilian staffers. Sitting next to me, Lacy Wright – who would turn out to be one of the real heroes in the final days of the war – whispered: "Jeeeesus Kee-rist, that guy can't even order off a Vietnamese monul"

The officers (half civilian, half military) in the field loved Vann and to many he must have seemed like a god swooping down from the sky. He would fly in, give them a pep talk and get them all fired up to feats of bravery, and then fly off again. Buildings like the Franzblau in Bien Hoa abounded in Vietnam, all named after a decade's worth of fallen heroes, some of them Vann's men. I often wonder how many of his men went down that foolhardy path that he would later himself follow.

Once at one of Vann's briefings for newcomers, I sat beside a fresh green major. Chatting before Vann entered, the "Newbie" said that he had heard about this Vann Vann Vann and had now seen him, but was not impressed. I merely smiled and let it go by. Just then, Vann strode into the room at his usual brisk pace, all jumped to their feet, and he started speaking before he even reached the rostrum. There he took up a pointer and indicated on the maps behind him the positions of the NVA and the ARVN. He rattled off statistics at machine-gun speed, summed up the current military situation, not only in the Delta but also in the other three Corps, and told us how we could win this war. He then dashed out with apologies that he had to get down country fast to "put out a fire". Within seconds we heard the sound of his chopper taking off.

It was a breathtaking performance, as usual, and the assembled newcomers sat stunned. The major turned to me with a dazed look on his face; I said, "That was John Paul Vann."

After the lecture, I heard him later say that he felt if Vann had said he wanted ten right arms, then the next day there would have arrived at Vann's headquarters the severed right arms of most of the men in the room. (He did not say if he would have been among them.) In retrospect all this seems hard to believe, but at that time and place Vann was a juggernaut and – we all thought – invincible.

Sometimes if Vann was up in Saigon, or on one of his rare leaves, Colonel Wilson would take the chopper for trips to the outposts. He would never take us along but Vann enjoyed taking us with him on short hops. I used to hear him tell visitors who had reservations about going on one of Vann's notorious low-level swoops over VC country, "Hell, my secretaries go out with me all the time." He loved gutsy females so we could pretty much write our own tickets. Everyone was armed in Vietnam and we were also issued pistols. The only time we ever fired them, luckily, was on the practice range where we honed our skill. And I would never have dreamed of carrying one with me – too heavy. Forget the "enemy", it was just too dangerous to me. I also did not relish the possibility of shooting myself in the foot – or elsewhere.

For chopper rides we had our own flight helmets with mikes and my call sign was Delta Queen. We did not have to wear flight suits or anything special but just clambered aboard in whatever we were wearing – and we never had any complaints. Vann ran his operation his way and few, outside the Saigon cabal, questioned him. I loved those tree-top rides over the Delta's lush green paddies and countryside with its canals and winding waterways. It was incredibly beautiful country and seemed untouched by war – but even amidst all this beauty the war had profoundly and tragically touched them all in one way or another: destruction, dislocation, lost loved ones, split families.

In some areas there had been saturation bombing by B-52s that had left large craters. In the low-lying Delta any hole rapidly filled with water so now the craters that dotted the fields served as wallows for water buffalo. As we flew low over them on my many gunboat chopper flights – we used choppers like we use taxis today – the submerged buffalo, only their backs, heads and horns showing, would look up lazily at us. When they were not submerged there was usually a small Vietnamese boy perched, or sometimes lying, on the buffalo's back. Sometimes at the end of a hot day, the buffaloes would be in a local stream with children swimming and splashing around them while the parents in their conical straw hats walked slowly home from their fields past the happy gathering of their children.

In response to a question I had once asked Vann – whether we gals could drive on an intermittently dangerous road – he had told us to go wherever we liked, and "have fun!" This gave me opportunities to see some pretty dodgy places during my tours in Vietnam. The stay in a Green Beret base camp up near the Cambodian border (or maybe in Cambodia, who knows?) was one of them, but that was not by car, and anyway was against all regulations so we need not go into that one.

The Navy also had a presence in the Delta and as Can Tho lay close to the Mekong, the swift-boat officers, known as the "River Rats", had a villa there. We used to go to their parties, and they rivaled even the Air Force in terms of food and other accoutrements. They had patrols and other dodgy doings in the waterways but, unlike the pilots, they never offered to take us on any rides so we were never quite sure what they were up to. Only later and by other means would we get to cruise local rivers.

While in Can Tho, my current pilot – I was serially monogamous – and I decided to spend the Christmas holiday in a small French hotel in Long Hai, down the coast from Vung Tau (the

French knew it as Cap St. Jacques). The French colonials had early on built their villas there and more recently the Vietnamese upper crust had done the same. Now these were all ghostly ruins, destroyed in the fighting that had seesawed back and forth in the area for years. The empty shells of lovely old villas were scattered along the hills overlooking the wide sweep of the bay.

The area was then Viet Cong-infested and considered by the military to be a dangerous drive but we drove down with an insouciant French couple who pooh-pooh'd the Americans' constant concerns for their safety. It was a lovely old hotel on a low bluff overlooking the bay and it even had a Christmas tree in the lobby. There was an ancient swimming pool that kept leaking water and they kept refilling it which kept it fairly clean and refreshingly cold. I think we were the only non-French guests there; we talked softly and tried to keep a low profile so as not to spoil their party.

There was spasmodically no electricity so after a leisurely day swimming, sitting around the pool under large canvas umbrellas or walking the paths along the bluff, we dined by candlelight on French food prepared by a Vietnamese chef who had been trained by the French. It was a poignant farewell feast for us – my pilot would soon be transferred back to the States – a memorable wartime interlude in a lovely setting that seemed so far from the war.

Well, maybe not so far after all. It got a bit closer when we tried to arrange our transport back to Saigon. We had been told we need only contact the Green Beret post nearby and could easily hitch a ride back into town – the usual means of getting anywhere in Vietnam (if there was no chopper available). What we had not counted on was that the road was considered too dangerous to drive at night, even the relatively short distance to Vung Tao. From there, we could always get a chopper ride or even take a military bus to Saigon, but how were we to get there?

We could not make much of a fuss as we knew we were not really allowed to be where we were; the area was not "pacified" and the hotel was strictly off-limits for the military. But we had to get back to Can Tho so we pleaded our case with the Green Berets: we were not Newbies, we did not mind taking a chance, blah blah blah. The snake-eaters were unimpressed; they had absolutely no intention of putting us, or themselves, on the road at night and that was that. We thus spent the extra night in the hotel, got a ride the next morning after first light, and somehow managed to get back to Can Tho – a bit late but without getting into trouble. Maybe the prevailing Christmas spirit helped us.

A few months later, another USAID gal and I decided to drive down to Rach Gia on the coast, an area famous for the *nuoc mam* fish sauce rendered nearby. We persuaded our pilots to drive down with us. The more deeply we drove into the less-pacified areas the more nervous they got. Many of the military never left their bases except to go to the local bars that had sprung up like mushrooms nearby. These two were definitely not happy travelers, especially when Rach Gia turned out to be not nearly as picturesque as we had hoped. The ambience was not enhanced by the stench of fermenting fish that lay all around us drying in the sun. The pilots were visibly relieved when we headed home and they never really relaxed until we drove through the air base gate again. They declined suggestions for further drives into the countryside and we thought we might have to resume viewing the Delta exclusively by air.

Luckily not. We were later flown down to a more southerly province in IV Corps for a party of some sort – of course in a plane sent on an "official" mission in the area. One of the activities the hosts had laid on for us visitors was a longboat ride down one of the smaller waterways that laced the area. We had a couple of armed USAID and military staffers with us and were lazily putt-putting along a narrow stretch under some dense overhead cover when a powerfully-motored longboat suddenly shot out of a side waterway a bit ahead of us. It turned left and passed us close enough that we could have leaned out and touched it. As it went by we saw that there were two men in it and that it was sitting very low in the water.

That was because it was stacked to the gunwales with heavy wooden ammo boxes bearing US Army markings. We looked at them and they looked at us – and we just let it go at that. We certainly did not want to get into a firefight with a Viet Cong supply team at this particular time and place – or ever. The VC always had the advantage of concealment and our side was almost always forced to fight at their chosen place and in the open. Luckily this was apparently not a place where they chose to interrupt their routine, or disrupt their secure supply line. We only wondered from which ARVN outpost their (and our) ammo had been stolen – or possibly purchased?

A trip by a bunch of girls, flown down to the farther reaches of the provinces to attend a party, was not an uncommon occurrence. In the interest of full disclosure, I should tell you here a bit more of what it was like to be a female searching for transportation to somewhere in Vietnam during the war.

In the period that I was in Vietnam, there were probably not more than twenty or so American females under the age of forty, and/or under two hundred pounds, we used to say (including military nurses and other agencies' staff, the number probably still didn't exceed a hundred). That helped provide us with great mobility. If we wanted to hop a ride up country we would just go out to the nearest air base or military facility that had a chopper company attached. We would find the dispatcher, or even a passing pilot, plead our case, usually successfully, and hop aboard.

We always flew Space-A (standby) and I assuage my conscience by telling myself that we almost never ever bumped some more deserving passengers. Or perhaps not… I hope not. I still retain a vision, however, of a Hispanic EM being shoved, protesting loudly, out a chopper door to make room for… someone.

We rode mostly in Hueys, both slicks and gunships, but we preferred the gunships because the doors were always open for the machine guns to swing out and downward, so we could lean out from the gunner's seat and see a lot more. We also occasionally caught a big Chinook "Flying Banana" but they offered virtually no visibility and with the twin rotors it was like riding a swaying and bouncy bus through noisy traffic.

Vann was a media magnet; there were a lot of war correspondents in Vietnam and not enough good stories to go around. There were always reporters in our office either waiting for him to show up or trying to pick up some Vann-related tidbit. I soon had some good friends in the hack pack. They and the pilots shared many similar characteristics, including smarts, a devil-may-care philosophy – plus most were party animals. (In my whole time in Vietnam, I don't think I ever dated outside that narrow double band, except for Dave, the CIA guy, who unfortunately had gotten killed early on.)

We would sometimes schedule our R&Rs on the same flights as our current loves. For these "Dirty Weekends", as we called them (some of which could stretch for longer on shared R&Rs), we often chose Hong Kong, not only because of its spectacular scenery and amenities but also for its shopping. But in that long-ago and more puritanical – well, at least outside of Asia – era, cohabiting with a non-spouse was not as easy as it is now. Registration at hotels with different names was always a problem. Once my pilot and I were checking in at the Hilton's front desk when a Washington acquaintance I had not seen for years spotted me and shrieked, "Why Tess Johnston, what are you doing here?!" She wanted to take me out to dinner and I told her to call me later; but by being registered under another name I managed to dodge that bullet.

On another occasion when we were staying at the posh Peninsula Hotel, it sent a Bentley to the airport to pick us up. Forgetting that we were in a British Crown Colony and hence an English-speaking city, we just assumed that our Chinese driver spoke no English. On the drive into Kowloon, we discussed at some length the best way to register. When we got to the hotel and pressed a generous tip into the chauffeur's hand he thanked us in flawless English, wished us a pleasant stay at the hotel and, I could have sworn, winked at us. But it could have just been a facial tic.

For the record, although there were usually attractive women in Vann's office or operations, he never touched any of us. He explained it succinctly to anyone who commented on this anomaly. "Never get your meat where you get your bread." And he never did. Part of the admiration that he enjoyed, especially among the men, was undoubtedly due to his reputed sexual prowess. In III Corps he always used to swear that a drive from Bien Hoa to Saigon took him only seventeen minutes – while it always took us at least half an hour. He was famous for picking up a local dolly, professional or amateur, to give her a ride to Saigon. He always claimed that a 'quickie' usually occurred en route. Unlike the males who were always in awe of Vann's swordsmanship, we gals figured that he must have been absolutely awful at it: maybe thirty seconds' worth of foreplay followed by a consummation of equal duration?

Vann really preferred Asian women – perhaps because he was short? – and they all seemed to adore him. He had, in addition to all his casual pick-ups, two full-time mistresses. In Saigon there was Lee, a Chinese-Vietnamese businesswoman, and then there was Annie, a very young Vietnamese whom he had met while she was still a school girl. He later set her up in a villa in Can Tho and one of our jobs was to keep the two mistresses apart – and in that we succeeded. Despite some near misses, they never knew about each other until after Vann's death. (A lot of other secrets then came out then too, but they are in another book, Neil Sheehan's *A Bright Shining Lie*, started in Vietnam in 1972 and finished some 16 years later.)

Here's how it worked: Vann and Colonel Wilson shared a long two-apartment hooch by the swimming pool in Palm Springs. Vann kept some of his clothes and toiletries there and even slept there some nights when he got in late or had an early takeoff the next morning. On the very rare occasions when Vann could not stop Lee from coming down to Can Tho, they both slept there. When she would call the office after hours, or when Vann was with Annie, someone would simply say that Vann was out in the field; he was gone so much that this was always plausible.

We only saw Annie occasionally when one of us was sent over to the rather modest villa (Vann's real residence, supplied him by the Vietnamese government at his request) to take her some supplies from the PX or to pick up something for him. When Vann went up to Saigon it was always on business so Annie had no reason to suspect he had another mistress there. The only really tense times were when Lee was in Can Tho and was not content to lounge around the Palm Springs pool but wanted to go places with Vann, places where they might be seen together. Everyone in his immediate office was in on the cover-up but outside it, Vann must have had enemies, and probably even Viet Cong, watching him. It is amazing that no one blew the whistle on him. If anyone had squealed on him we certainly would have known about it, because we figured that Lee would have killed him.

Did we approve of all this? I don't remember even thinking about it. Vann's unbridled sexual pursuits were just part of the total package. There was a war on, people died all around you. "The World" was very far away, and somehow normal rules didn't seem to apply. For instance, every senior officer for whom I worked, and indeed almost every civilian one I knew, had a Vietnamese girlfriend or mistress, the latter often being totally supported by the man. Other than Colonel Wilson there may have been other "Straight Arrows" in the country – but I did not personally know any of them.

The Americans regularly took their paid "family visitation leaves" to see their wives in the US or in one of the designated family or "safe-haven" posts in the surrounding Asian countries. They then came back to work – and back into the arms of their live-ins. But it is interesting that most of these extramarital relationships turned out to be durable. After Vietnam fell, almost all the Vietnamese girlfriends wound up in the US – and almost all the men I knew later divorced their wives and married their Vietnamese lovers.

Many of these clever and industrious Vietnamese women later made some of their rather lackluster husbands rich by establishing bakeries, restaurants and other successful businesses. In the long run, the Vietnamese mistresses turned out to be good value for money and, as we also say of Chinese immigrants to the United States, they and their children enriched the gene pool.

This might be a good place to mention that even we women had some contacts with Vietnamese, but aside from the few females in our offices, mostly only those in the higher echelons. Vann would have parties for such people as local officials, professionals and businessmen. As they tended to be mostly males, he often invited a few of us females, perhaps as window dressing or just to lend some light to all that sameness of uniforms and dark suits. Sometimes the Vietnamese civilians brought along their wives (but unless they lived in Can Tho, the military officers didn't do so, as their wives were often back in the family home elsewhere with their children).

I got to know several Vietnamese including a lovely family, a doctor and his wife and growing children, and even got invited to their homes for dinner. There was almost inevitably a "hidden agenda" in these friendships; maybe items from the PX, recommendations for access to someplace or someone, that sort of thing. I did not mind this (and usually was of little help to them anyway) as I felt it was simply an exchange: I got to know them a bit, see how they lived, the interiors of lovely old villas – and often what exceptional cooks they had – in return for a few inconsequential favors.

In the course of one evening's dinner, I had visited my hosts' bathroom to "freshen up" (literally, as often the major rooms had ceiling fans rather than air conditioning) and I remember looking in the mirror of their rather modern, inset medicine cabinet over the wash basin. A decade later in California, I met the wife again and she asked me if I ever wanted to go back to Vietnam. I told her that I might at some future date, who knows? She then gave me their villa's address and said if I ever did go to Can Tho, I should try to get into their villa (a farfetched idea at best), go into the bathroom, pry open that inlaid medicine cabinet and looks for gold bars lined top to bottom behind. I wonder if perhaps some North Vietnamese official had already had a lucky day and suddenly become a rich man?

Another of my local friends was my Vietnamese language tutor. Trong was a Vietnamese Army Lieutenant who, like all his fellow officers, earned less than a living wage. He supplemented his meager income not with corruption (which was common) but with tutoring, both in Vietnamese and French. Like many Vietnamese of his age and class, he had studied in a French primary, secondary and then law school. I must admit that I did not learn a great deal of Vietnamese because he was so cultured (and of course fluent in English) that our conversation ranged widely and language study fell by the wayside. After spending long hours together we became friends and I was able to help him in some small ways (besides paying more than the going rate for language lessons). Later, however, I was able to repay him in a much more important way, and I did so for a long period.

After the defeat of South Vietnam, he and his fellow officers were sent (with no equipment of any kind) to remote countryside sites to set up a camp using mostly their bare hands. They somehow managed to survive and were interned there for nearly a decade. I no longer remember how, but I had gotten a mailing address to which packages could be sent to him. During that long incarceration in the most primitive of conditions, I sent packages at intervals – medicines, non-perishable foods, pencils and ballpoint pens – each package varied. I was always hoping I had chosen something that he really needed (or as he told me much later, that he could swap with the NVA guards for more food or favors).

After a decade or so he finally was released and was able to get to the United States to join some of his family members who had managed to get out far earlier. He married a Vietnamese and started – far too late and in fragile health – a new life in a suburb of Washington. Like all of the thirty family members now in the US that he helped sponsor, they are all professionals, their children and now grandchildren scattered throughout the US and Canada.

On my "Home Leaves" later, I lived quite near to him and would visit him and talk about our lives in Vietnam. I also once asked him which of my packages had been of the most use and without hesitation he said it was the ones with medicines, because so many of the guards had venereal diseases and he could trade the pills for things of greatest value. I had sent some of my later packages while serving in the German Democratic Republic (GDR, or East Germany, a fellow communist country), and there I had gotten a little bolder. Whereas I had been careful before – as I knew all packages would be opened by GDR officials but that medicines and foodstuffs would be allowed through and probably not be pilfered – in one of the last packages before being assigned to another post, I sent him a photo of me in a frame. And between some of the layers of cardboard that held it in place, I slipped a US$20 bill. I just hoped it would get through – and I now asked him if it had.

He said it was the greatest package he ever received, because (even though he said the guards carefully tore even the cardboard boxes apart) the bill had gotten through. And he traded it (in the jungle of Vietnam!) for life-saving items. He said he was sorry I had not tried that sooner, and I could have shot myself for not having done so.

My dear old friend, Ngo Trung Trong, died last year surrounded by his loving local family and mourned by far-flung family members now on several continents. I was privileged to know him and will always treasure his friendship. I am only grateful that, thanks to a lucky break, I was in a place at a time when I could make his life a bit easier in some small way.

Back to the other realities of war. We had local flare-ups down in the Delta but after I arrived I can recall no big sustained campaigns like the ones farther north. We lost some good men, mostly due to chopper malfunctions, a frequent killer. In my seven years in Vietnam I lost eleven colleagues, friends and acquaintances; one by assassination, and the other ten in airplane or chopper crashes.

One was a brilliant young West Pointer, himself the son of a West Pointer, and with a great Army career ahead of him. He had fought heroically alongside Vann in the Delta some nine years earlier. He was a favorite of Vann and of us all – he was a really great guy. His chopper malfunctioned and went down into the river and neither he nor his crew survived. When Vann heard the news he immediately jumped into his chopper and flew down to the crash site, circled over the spot, and dispatched men at once to recover the bodies. But it was too late; by the time they got there, the bodies in the water had already been stripped of their wallets, watches and rings.

A popular and effective Province Senior Advisor, also a West Pointer, was another of Vann's brave men. He was ambushed while traveling down a waterway in the lower Delta. Mad as a hornet, armed and lusting for blood, Vann flew up and down the canal at treetop level trying to spot the VC who had ambushed him, but as usual they were long gone; they always struck and then managed to fade into the lush cover of the countryside. Then, in that same awful period, yet another of our Province Senior Advisors, with whom we had worked more closely in our office, was also killed. It was an irony that so many were killed now that the war was – theoretically at least – winding down.

About the time of the NVA's Easter Offensive of March 1972, Vann transferred up to II Corps to take over as Senior American Advisor, the highest-ranking civilian there and indeed the first non-military officer ever to hold that job, before or after. I remained in IV Corps working for Colonel Wilson, who took over there, but it was considerably less exciting now without Vann and the coterie of correspondents who followed him everywhere, always eager to pick his brain after any US policy shift, major local battle or other critical event. Wilson was equally well-informed, never minced his words, and could also be counted on to provide pithy quotes, but he simply did not have Vann's ambition, charisma or flair in handling the press pack; also, he just couldn't be bothered.

Then on June 9, 1972, the unthinkable happened. The invincible, immortal John Paul Vann was killed in II Corps near Pleiku. In the darkness, zooming low over a highway recklessly as ever, to taunt the VC who were entrenched along that route, his chopper slammed into a stand of tall trees and exploded. His body was found, broken but unburned, at the base of the trees.

Ironically, those were the only tall trees left in this slash-and-burn area. They were there because the local Montagnards left them standing to protect the graves of their ancestors buried beside them. Vann had always admired these sturdy, brave mountain people and now he lay among them. He had lived an incredibly full life, adventurous and action-packed, but he was only forty-seven years old when he died. No one could ever have imagined Vann as an old man, but we had somehow believed in his mantle of immortality. We were all numb with shock and grief.

In the vast hall at the memorial service in Saigon, the crowd far overflowed all the available space. I looked at the faces of the many men who owed their careers to Vann; they had now lost their mentor, protector and invincible leader – as had we all. So many hopes and dreams died with John Paul Vann. I was not at the Vann funeral in the United States, so I will let Neil Sheehan describe the event: "It was like an extraordinary class reunion. Here were all the figures from Vietnam in the chapel. General Westmoreland was the chief pallbearer. Also in attendance were such diverse individuals as Edward Lansdale, Lucien Conein, Daniel Ellsberg, Edward Kennedy, pro-war columnist Joseph Alsop, Robert Komer and William Colby."

Not long thereafter, Colonel Wilson went back to the US for consultations with some of the big brass. After a particularly contentious meeting with one of the top ones he returned to his quarters and suffered a fatal heart attack. In a sense he died in battle, although not with the Viet Cong. In helping to ship Wilson's effects from Vietnam. I became good friends with his sister Eugenia, a warm and wonderful woman whom I grew to know and love and who later visited me in four Foreign Service posts. Perhaps that was Colonel Wilson's legacy to me.

Vann was buried at Arlington National Cemetery and Colonel Wilson next to him – comrades in death as in life.

Within 48 hours of Colonel Wilson's death, his job was taken over by his deputy. As he had his own secretary, I now had no job and USAID Personnel in Saigon suddenly had to find a place for me. Thanks to my reputation – and, I suspect, my having worked for both Vann and Colonel Wilson – I had some Brownie points on my record there. There were, however, no jobs open in the field right then and I definitely did not want to serve in Saigon. But I only had to wait in limbo for a short period for something to turn up.

In the interim, I will dwell a little longer on Can Tho, in the interval after Vann went up to II Corps. Colonel Wilson was still my boss but serving now as the DEPCORDS. We worked with the same staff, and at a pace perhaps more typical of a CORDS post. But now, without Vann, a little of the spark had gone out of it.

11

A DAY OF DUTY IN THE DELTA

Can Tho was a pleasant – but less exciting – change from the Tet and post-Tet mortaring and rocketing we had experienced in Bien Hoa, very different from the world of Vann, our dynamo. But as it was the support and command post for IV Corps' provinces, even without him, we were kept busy. The following is a description of a typical day in the wartime Delta after Vann's departure.

THE "PALM SPRINGS" compound is beautiful and quiet at 0630 in the morning when I let the dogs out. The torrential downpour of last night that made a steady roar on the tin roof of my hooch has washed down everything, and a faint warm mist rises from the ground. All of our Singapore pre-fab hooches in the compound are low long buildings with overhanging eaves and tin roofs. Even if not elegant, painted white and surrounded by luxuriant flowers and palm trees, they fit nicely into their tropical setting. Each day as I leave for work, I note the rapid growth of the papaya tree planted only a few months ago, now halfway to my shoulders and already with large glossy leaves.

Just outside the compound wall my favorite stand of bamboo is now taller than the two-storey house it partially shades. As I sit by the pool and look in any direction, I see bamboo, palm and papaya trees, bougainvillea, and gladiola as tall as people, trailing vines with blooms that look like big blue morning glories and spiky green plants with sharp points that inflict painful pricks if you walk into them in the dark. The "moat" out front of the compound used to be filled with the loveliest of water flowers that were open early in the morning and closed tight when you came home at night. But now that the road has been widened, they have disappeared and we have only an ugly, smelly drainage ditch that rapidly fills in the torrential rains and thus can never be covered – a pretty poor substitute for those lovely flowers.

I get the dogs launched on their usual morning rat hunt and return to my hooch to start the coffee. The maid will not come in until after I leave the house at 0725, so I just ignore last night's dirty dishes and disarray. Since the morning is cool, I turn off the air-con and open the windows of my bedroom that faces the compound's pool and small garden beyond my parked car.

I must keep the curtains drawn at night as the pair of guards patrol past the building at half hour intervals, chatting away in their high nasal sing-song. I am sure they would be enthralled at a glimpse of my strange existence in a room filled nearly wall-to-wall with a gigantic water bed; I live my entire off-duty life in this one room and do my reading there. I even taught my Maryland University classes while lolling on it when the number of students dwindled to the four hardy souls who could fit onto my room with only a small sofa and single chair. My second or "front" room serves as kitchen, dining room, bridge-playing room and dog dormitory. It is separated from this larger room by a window, as my kitchen used to be a porch. While the water boils, I turn on the radio for the morning AFN news, our only up-to-date contact with the outside world except for the *Stars and Stripes*, the Army newspaper that comes down from Saigon, often a day late.

The shower alternately scalds and freezes me so I know that someone is also taking a shower in his bathroom in the center core of the four units that make up our hooch. Later through the ventilation opening in the ceiling, I can also hear him gargling. And the dividing wall that backs up my bed is so thin that I can hear my next-door neighbor coughing in his bed; luckily he and I both are quiet creatures and keep our music down low. Despite our cozy proximity, I have never had a complaint and nor has he, which probably indicates what boring people we are.

The morning's AFN news is repetitious, as is almost every morning's lately – small gains, small losses, great hopes. A mine disaster in Africa killed several hundred but in the war here only two Americans and yet unnumbered Vietnamese are reported killed. I check the day's weather forecast. We are currently transitioning into the monsoon season and I may have to change shoes (and probably clothes) several times today; it is far too hot and sticky to wear a raincoat and getting in and out of cars under an umbrella in a torrential downpour is not so easy. Tropical rains are real frog-chokers and I know I'll get soaked even if I park within a few feet of the door at each end of the journey. I gulp down my coffee, shove the dogs into the kitchen to await the maid and quickly slide out the door before they can follow me.

By now our compound parking lot is half-empty and the guards have swung open the big metal gates that stay closed all night. They salute snappily and smile as I drive through; they probably don't like me any better than anyone else, but I give them American cigarettes when no one is looking. In return, they come running to me when my two dogs (of the seven that live in the compound) get into trouble or try to get out of the gate. Traffic at this morning hour is heavy, headed both out to the military bases and into town from the countryside. It ranges from bicycles to huge military "six-bys" – the trucks that menace life and limb as they speed down the middle of the road with lights on and air-horns blaring. (It is often observed by us that if the

Vietnamese fought as aggressively as they drove, this war would have been over years ago.)

Indigenous to Can Tho is a new version of the Saigon cyclo; only here, the passenger sits in back of the bicycle and is pulled along in a sort of metal rickshaw as opposed to the Saigon version where the passenger serves as bumper in a seat projecting out in front. The latter is delightful to travel in: you sit under the canopy, the driver above and behind you on the bicycle. You are propelled silently through the streets with only the swish of the tires on the asphalt and the grunts of exertion from the driver to disturb you as you weave in and out of Saigon's heavy and menacing motorized traffic. In Can Tho, private cars are not very common; bicycles and motorbikes prevail and the din is unbelievable. Every male in our Phong Dinh Province must have a Honda – often laden with a wife and one to four children (six aboard is the record sighting), or perhaps two ARVN buddies – all weaving with foolhardy élan in and out of the congested traffic.

With the help of the intrepid guard – who weighs about eighty pounds and waves a sort of ping-pong paddle with the word "STOP" on it – I succeed in pulling out into the heavy traffic. I must inch out bit by bit until they must stop or crash into me. Even then, they continue to maneuver around me on either side, often swinging far out into the opposite lane or riding up over the curbing to get around me. Left turn finally negotiated, I head toward the office five blocks away. There are Hondas and bicycles passing on either side and it is not uncommon for a local "cowboy" on a motorbike to try to snatch off your watch as he swings by your open car window.

Ahead of me, traffic has slowed behind a cart full of bricks pulled by a gnarled man of at least seventy and pushed by a young boy. The man has a wide web strap around his forehead as he pulls on the shanks of the cart and the boy helps guide it by leaning his full weight against one side and then the other. The pace is agonizingly slow and they are drenched in sweat, fairly rare in the Vietnamese, who perspire much less than we Caucasians.

We get around him only to be slowed by a well-worn bus with people hanging on its sides and the top covered with mounds of vegetable sacks and some ducks peering at the passing parade from their crowded cage. The bus has been unsuccessful in making a U-turn in this busy traffic and now is crosswise in the road with the traffic allowing it to neither back up nor go forward. Amidst blaring horns plus hand directions by the "pusher" – a lad whose job is to shove people in the bus door and to toss their bundles onto the top – finally the turn-around is negotiated and once again traffic flows in its own disorderly fashion.

In addition to the *cyclos*, bikes, Hondas and the large intra-provincial buses, the most ubiquitous sight is the "tri-Lambretta," a three-wheeled motor scooter with a little covered cabin where the driver sits, often flanked by a passenger on each side, and with a small passenger compartment on the back that will hold maybe ten Vietnamese (or four Americans) sitting on low benches facing each other. When it rains, plastic curtains are rolled down over the open sides to give passengers partial protection. Often this invaluable vehicle is leased to the driver or else is his only possession and thus is also his home. At night you see them parked, a hammock slung crosswise in the back, the side curtains pulled down and the driver asleep with his useful possessions, perhaps a towel, a bowl, a shirt and a poncho tucked under his head as a pillow. Since he may have no family nearby to cook for him, he too will be a steady customer at the numerous mobile *pho* soup stands that feed us all.

As the GI trade dwindles in the current drawdown, the drivers must fight increasingly for customers. They cluster around the doors of the more popular bars trying to lure a GI to ride back to the base with them; they can make more money from one GI than from 10 Vietnamese passengers who pay only a few Piasters for the ride, while a GI may pay a hundred or more, depending on how drunk, generous or clueless he is.

These mobile workhorses stop when hailed at either side of the road – or often right in the middle – and pull out again with total disregard for any traffic behind them (the rearview mirrors are mostly missing), thus forming yet another major traffic hazard. They can also be hired to transport household goods, foodstuffs or just about anything else. One day, I followed some fat pink pigs, feet trussed and lying on the floor of the narrow passenger aisle and loudly, squealing in protest. In the mornings, the back is full of children going to school or housewives going to market.

The produce they buy was probably picked in the nearby countryside the night before, the fish caught that morning and the pigs, chickens and ducks brought in to the market still alive. The latter are then killed right on the spot to cater to the demands of customers who don't want to carry the live fowl home. I once saw a man on a bicycle with at least twenty live ducks, trussed together by the feet in pairs and hung over a bamboo pole running the length of the bike, all craning their heads and together protesting on this, their "Last Ride".

Can Tho lies along the Bassac River with a ferry site on its northern boundary. There are two ferries that one crosses between it and Saigon, which is what consumes your driving time to Saigon, a trip that would take only two hours with no ferries but takes about five hours, with luck, including the crossings. Ben Xe Moi means, literally "New Bus Station" but connotes that area of Can Tho that has come to life since the arrival of the

GIs in the Delta. Its prime thoroughfare is lined on both sides by girlie bars and Indian shops featuring merchandise catering to the more basic tastes of their GI customers.

The few tailors (one appropriately named Hart, Shaffner & Marks, which must have its namesakes spinning in their graves) feature displays of African dashikis and the multi-pocketed 'safari' suits. By early afternoon, the bar girls lean in the doorways of the bars and bordellos or sit on stools on the streets plucking at any GIs who passes by. Peanut sellers, little girls who are barely of kindergarten age, cluster around a GI and pick at him, one slightly older one (probably the boss) working on his back-pocket wallet while the others create the diversion. The more daring pickpockets slash pockets with razor blades and it's a common sight to see GI's uniforms sewed up neatly along the pocket lines by the "mama-sans" who do their laundry.

On payday night, fights are frequent, men with men, girls with men, girls with girls, and the Military Police (or White Mice) have a busy night with the paddy wagon. This morning it is quiet, with the few GIs who managed to evade the curfew and spend the night downtown trying to inconspicuously hail a *cyclo* to return to the base. A few girls lean out of second-storey windows or stretch lazily on the balconies, but most of them are not even up yet (or have perhaps spent the night with their families since the advent of a curfew). The Indian shops are not yet open as they know the GIs will not begin to filter into town until about noon. A street sweeper wearing a straw hat kicks a piece of debris into his scoop with his bare splayed foot; it may take him all day to traverse the length of the street.

In the morning sunlight it is a cheerful scene despite the dirt and shabbiness of the buildings. Vietnamese stores and houses are made entirely of cement – the more elegant version, that is, as opposed in the poorer fringes of the city and made of nipa palm or flattened sheets of tin cans advertising Budweiser or Shasta Cola. The basic architecture is a long shoebox affair, perhaps with a shop in the front and the family's quarters behind a partition or curtain about halfway back. The local hotels are often the same design, with the living room or lobby in the front, kitchen in the back, rooms upstairs and a bath tacked on the very back, if not completely outdoors. The middle rooms often lack windows but have open designs in a wooden room divider at ceiling level where light can filter through. There is seldom glass in the windows, but at the front almost always an ornate iron grill, either gaily painted or left to rust. The floors are tile, which is fortunate since the gutters often overflow in the monsoon season and it is a common sight in the monsoon season to see the lady of the house sweeping water out the door.

Furniture is minimal but (in town, at least) usually consists of a large wooden bed and on a hot night straw mats laid down to sleep on. Usually there is a wardrobe, often with a glass or mirrored door, where the family's most prized possessions are kept. Hammocks made of hemp or canvas are also popular as they can be strung almost anywhere. The string one also serves as an ideal cradle as it is airy and cool and envelops the child securely in the mesh while the mother rocks it with her foot while doing the family chores with her free hands.

In our office district, houses are scarcer with most of the "high rent" space occupied by income-producing shops or bars. In the early morning hours, the fruit and cold drink stands have not been rolled out yet but even now some ambitious soup sellers are already heating water on charcoal braziers set up by the curb. At night after the curfew has cleared the street of GIs, the warm glow of many of these little stoves draws people to them to sit around and talk or eat.

The CORDS Headquarters consists of two former hotels,

three storeys high and behind a wall topped by barbed wire. There is a parking lot and atop the taller of the two buildings, the DEPCORDS' chopper pad from which all flights take off. His pilot lives in the building and is never more than a minute away from his chopper. Proximity to the office is essential for the chopper and its pilot and in this congested area only rooftops offer space for a landing pad.

Turning left into the compound against the stream of traffic once again occupies my complete attention as we have one or two accidents per week at this critical juncture. Often a car sitting perfectly still will be rammed from behind by a truck or jeep (the latter if you are lucky), and once a Honda, its passenger looking backwards for some unexplained reason, crashed into the back of a stationery car at full force, sending the rider sailing onto the roof of the car. He brushed himself off, went back to retrieve his Honda, and was able to drive off on it.

As I turn in, I must stop halfway through the gate for the security inspection: the car hood is lifted to search for planted bombs and a guard with a mirror much like a large dentist's mirror walks around the car looking underneath it for explosives. We are encouraged to keep our car windows rolled up to prevent grenades being thrown in – but that happened quite some time ago (five in one day, three vehicles destroyed but no fatalities). Now both the passengers and the guards have become lax and everything will remain perfunctory until the next series of incidents. The guards find my car acceptable and I drive to my special parking spot just outside the office's front door. The duty officer, who has been here all night at his desk in the lobby, waves as I pass. Now he can turn over to me the duty log, his weapon and flashlight, and go home.

I examine the log and will later call any pertinent offices to solve problems that arose during the night: the chopper pad lights were out, a drunken American sergeant barged through the gate and refused to show his ID –just the usual routine stuff today. The log also shows incidents during the night in the provinces if there were major actions or KIAs. These go on a special incident report form and are scanned when they come in by Colonel Wilson and the province's Military Senior Advisor, although he will probably already have been briefed at the daily Generals' briefing held in the ARVN compound at 0630 or at the American briefing held at 0800 over at military HQ.

The maid has gotten to the office before me so all the air conditioners are on and the smell of coffee greets me. She operates out of a small room behind the office where we have a refrigerator, sink, coffee bar and, neatly tucked into one corner, the ladies' toilet. This makes for a cozy if not too private arrangement. We can keep anything we want in the fridge but things have a tendency to disappear so we limit it mostly to ice and things bought for consumption that day. Then I go into Colonel Wilson's office and open the two safes which contain the classified material neatly stored in several In-Boxes.

The office must now remain "secure" so I cannot leave it for any reason unless another American office mate comes to relieve me. At about 0745 Miss Hanh, our chief secretary/ receptionist will come in and at 0800 Mr Soan, the interpreter/translator, and Miss Ngu, the typist for our two military officers. This brings our happy little band up to nine. Ba Sau, who virtually lives in the pantry and caters to our every whim, pads around barefoot, usually with a damp rag in her hand to take periodic swipes at the dirt and dust that encroach on us in the dry season from under the doors or are tracked in on the many combat boots.

When it rains she has yet another job, as the office is almost level with the parking lot so the water seeps in under the door. Occasionally the pump in the back passageway fails and water begins to back up there. A pile of sandbags sits outside in the passageway at the back – not only for defense but to serve us in water emergencies.

Almost every day, we have a workman in the office repairing something that has broken down or shoring up something that is falling down, and we also have an electrician and carpenter on call. Since the buildings are concrete shells and we built in false ceilings, wood-paneled walls, etc., they serve as a natural home for termites and other bugs, which we have with us always. When the panels buckle from dampness, termite gnawing and/or jungle rot, we replace them one at a time. This makes a nice ongoing project for our General Service Officers when they are not ripping out faulty wiring or replacing dead phones. We never lack for lots of work projects in the offices.

When Colonel Wilson comes in, we immediately launch on a series of telephone calls to the provinces, Miss Hanh and I working simultaneously on our two telephones and at full voice trying to complete at least one call before Colonel Wilson must leave for the briefing. We shout in Vietnamese and English, curse, plead, get cut off, get wrong numbers, cannot hear the answering party, they cannot hear us, and we finally get it all cured. Then Colonel Wilson gets cut off after his first two words, he bellows from his office and we curse and start the process all over again. In the meantime, Miss Hanh gets a second call through, and right in the middle of that conversation my call is reconnected, frantic signals to Colonel Wilson that we now have the first call again, but he is still in the middle of the other one, so we ask our party to hold. He finishes one call and returns to ours which by now is cut off again; another bellow, another attempt. And so it goes.

The phone system is a cross which we all have to bear. There are sixteen provinces in the Delta and our only reliable link with them – if it could be called reliable – is through a complicated

telephone system, part-American and part-Vietnamese. It sput-
ters and crackles, goes dead, voices come through distorted or
broken, or fade out completely, leaving you talking to nobody.
Missing about every other word, you keep screaming "say
again!" into the phone, find that they can hear you perfectly and
loudly and you are deafening them, while you can hear nothing faint voices under a high buzz. When you are trying to get
a piece of work finished and you are told to contact a province,
your heart sinks because you know you must lay aside the work
and give your undivided attention to the time-consuming task.

On a busy day it gets more and more maddening and coro-
nary-provoking. Colonel Wilson went to a briefing over at Army
Headquarters one day when the Commo Officer was giving a
briefing. He informed his listeners that the telephone system was
highly effective and one of the best in Vietnam. They say Colonel
Wilson nearly fell off his chair and then informed the poor guy of
our daily telephone battles in terms so vivid that the officer still
has not recovered. Now, on days when we can't get through to
more than one or two provinces – which is virtually every day –
we send a memo to the Commo Officer outlining in detail dates,
times and our difficulties. It is reported that there are stacks of
complaints on the officer's desk – and he dodges into doorways
when he sees Colonel Wilson approaching.

What really drives us up the wall in the midst of a telephone
problems, however, is the frequent calls we get, and often at the
busiest times, from jerks who ask us what time the snack bar
closes, or for the telephone number of some obscure office. Since
our boss has the equivalent rank of a major-general (while we
secretaries are merely majors), we ask false-sweetly, "Would you
call a general's office to ask him such a stupid question?" But the
calls continue, often from the same party (one an alcoholic sergeant who has our number), and in desperation we sent all offic-

es a stack of phone books. That barely slows them down as they are too lazy to look up the numbers themselves. We only await the day when someone will call and ask us to pass a message to Big Lucy, the bar girl down the street. It would not surprise us.

We even got a call the other day asking us when we were going to get the grass cut in front of the Can Tho Airfield (definitely not our problem). We assured the caller that if he would go stand out in front of the airfield gate (in the sun at high noon), we would send a truck full of men and lawnmowers out immediately – "now you be sure to wait out there for them…"

Our calls are now completed or abandoned as Colonel Wilson has left for his morning briefing. I turn to the morning's documents, sort them according to urgency or importance and distribute them to the staff in the front office. Calls come in and visitors are dispatched to the proper offices. The front office is a clearing house for every sort of problem, many of which can usually be solved elsewhere. We get bewildered ARVN messengers and saffron-robed monks, Vietnamese couriers bringing in the morning's newspapers for our interpreter to translate, excerpt and analyze, officers from other divisions trying to track down lost documents, get signatures, set up appointments, plead their case for some cause, or get a cup of coffee and some TLC from one of Vietnamese secretaries. If we are having a bad morning, they often quickly back away.

One day we had two fresh-in-country majors waiting to meet Colonel Wilson. They sat saucer-eyed on the couch as he chewed out some poor miscreant at the top of his lungs while Miss Hanh screamed "You crazy!" into the telephone. They finally got up the nerve to ask if perhaps they should come back later. We assured them it would not be any better later and they reluctantly sat back down to wait for their appointed time slot. When Colonel Wilson finally received them, he was as soft-voiced as a turtle

dove and they were visibly relieved. Miss Hanh, in the meantime, had slammed down the phone in exasperation and the
whole office was suddenly serenely quiet.

While we wait for Colonel Wilson to return, Miss Hahn
takes off her sandals and polishes her long, pointed toenails, her
small feet looking like tiny manicured children's hands. If I get a
chance, I might get a glimpse at our morning *Stars and Stripes* –
but if I do, I will surely get ribbed for never having anything to
do in the front office.

I look through the days' predictions and put the "hot" ones
on top of the stack, to be read first. I note with particular interest
the ones that concern our province, or Can Tho itself, but they
are pretty tame. I get last week's DEPCORDS Sit-Reps out of the
file and lay them on Colonel Wilson's desk so that he can begin
to dictate the new one that is due every Monday evening in HQ
MACV in Saigon. It can run to many pages and I will be called
upon to do it at the last possible moment and there will be no
time to redraft.

A call comes in from Ca Mau about some Viet Cong action
of last night and they wish to make a spot report. I take out the
proper form and fill in the needed information: Who did what to
whom, where and with what? KIAs, WIAs, MIAs? Weapons captured? Any US personnel involved? So far this month we have
been lucky with no American KIA or WIA but it is not always so.
Some of our provinces are so secure that we can drive the roads
at any time; others are not secure and the US advisory efforts are
confined to small enclaves. One province is currently threatened
with NVA and VC troops within its borders. We know where
they are but the terrain is so hostile that no one will go out beyond the armed compound to confront the enemy; they must
stay and wait until they are hit first. The report I take is a minor
action so I lay it on the Military Senior Advisor's desk rather

than Colonel Wilson's.

Colonel Wilson comes in the front door and strides into his office, calling out several names of people whom he wishes to see at once. Miss Hahn and I get on the phone and notify the chosen few. A summons from Colonel Wilson's office is known to strike terror in even the most stalwart heart but I can tell by his tone that there is no crisis and I inform them accordingly. Almost before I have completed the last call the first officer comes in the door; I wave him into Colonel Wilson's office and close the door. The exchange is loud but not particularly heated; his usual tone of voice is loud. The man emerges with furrowed brow, scribbling in his notebook. Colonel Wilson is also known for giving elliptic instructions and as his mind races ahead of his mouth there are sometimes gaps to be bridged. He leaps from mountain top to mountain top and if you don't know what is down in the valleys, you're in trouble. This man is obviously plumbing those valleys as he leaves, muttering to himself.

We have a neat intercom system between all the offices but Colonel Wilson refuses to use it, so all instructions come from his desk that sits in an office about six feet from my desk. If I keep alert I can catch his every word, but if I don't then I too must reconstruct from surmises. Now he wants the pilot to be ready to take off from the rooftop in ten minutes. He will fly to four provinces today and when he knows which ones, I can call ahead and warn them of his impending arrival, which is bound to result in a flurry of activity. He has an unerring eye for spotting problems and weaknesses coupled with an impatience with those who don't have ready answers so his arrival is about as welcome as Attila the Hun's, especially in some of the less well-run provinces. As I tell our Newbies, Colonel Wilson does not tolerate fools gladly.

Today he reels off where he is going: Ba Xuyen, Bac Lieu, An

Xuyen and Chuong Thien, the latter our most insecure province. There he will be welcomed and his combat expertise and sound advice may make a difference in some future engagement. Dressed in wash khaki pants, a white poplin short-sleeve shirt (tailored in Hong Kong) and combat boots, he has only to throw on his blue nylon sailing jacket and a soft-brimmed hat and he is ready to fly. Because he has flown over almost every mile of the Delta dozens of times he knows unerringly where he wants to land, even if the pilot does not. His pilot – also named Wilson, to add to the confusion – says that when he is flying in the wrong direction or slightly off course, Colonel Wilson will simply indicate with his forearm the direction to fly and if Pilot Wilson will steer in a line with that direction they will arrive right on target.

I ring the bell on the roof (or in the pilot's room where he is on 24/7 standby), but he is already at work, busy pre-flighting the chopper. I go outdoors into the parking lot then give him our usual five fingers sign indicating five minutes to lift off and he gives me the thumb- up.

Between us, we have worked out an extensive array of signals which can indicate start up, shut down, wait ten, come down, go home, no passengers but take off anyway or – in desperation if Colonel Wilson suddenly disappears – the "I don't know what's going on, do you?" sign. We used to have a telephone right inside the door leading to the chopper pad but people kept picking it up trying to use it to make outside calls. That drove us crazy in the office, as it is a closed circuit and buzzed down there. The problem was neatly solved when someone simply cut the wire. We never had it restrung.

But as I watch Colonel Wilson walk out the door I already know the pilot will have the rotors going by the time he climbs the three flights of stairs and that they can take off immediately. It always thrills me to see the chopper lift off the roof and climb vertically and forward above the streets. It's even more thrilling from inside it (on the treasured occasions when we females are invited to fly) as we lift off with a nose-down whoop over the street and then veer off, climbing.

Often in the early part of the flight, Colonel Wilson will fall asleep and begin to lean toward one side or the other. Even without glancing over, the pilot can always tell when this happens as the small LOH will begin to lean in the direction Colonel Wilson leans – they are that sensitive to weight changes. Sometimes they will be fired on from the ground as they drop into small outposts far from the more pacified population centers. And sometimes Colonel Wilson returns with mud up to his knees from having landed near swampy ground or in a paddy and having to slog out to firmer ground. He is usually exhausted when he returns around 1700 hours – after all, he is 63 years old – so we seldom work beyond 1830 at night. Today, he indicates he will not return until 1730 so I may have to work late unless he has a dinner or a late HQ special briefing to attend. They tend to start early because of the 2130 curfew now in place.

Now that Colonel Wilson is gone, things settle down again and I have only his deputy and two light colonels to worry about. But they are "house-broken," as we say in the trade, meaning well-organized and unflappable, and unless the work load is tremendous we will putt-putt along steadily all day, mostly on routine matters (the high-powered stuff comes from Wilson himself) such as Sit-Reps, personnel actions, or answering questions from the field.

If it is really critical we will track down Colonel Wilson by telephone or radio; we have a Buffalo radio and field phone as a standby to all sixteen provinces but as we know that will not be all that easy. Just as Vann did when he was still here, if there is enemy action Colonel Wilson will leave his planned itinerary and fly down to where the action is, if possible often landing while it is still in progress, to assess the situation. But so far, not a peep out of him or the pilot. Today is quiet, broken only occasionally by the shudder of the windowpanes – always in three waves – from a high-flying B-52 strike somewhere in the countryside nearby. We go outdoors and see high above us the planes heading downriver. It must be a terrifying experience for those underneath them – but usually the only damage is to leave the "buffalo wallow" craters in the fields and paddies.

At 1130 it is time for my lunch, that I will probably eat in the office in order to be able to spend most of my lunch hour beside the pool. I give Ba Sau some Piasters and she takes my soup bowl across the street to the little Vietnamese soup stand that caters to *cyclo* drivers and CORDS' local employees. She has the bowl filled with my favorite *pho* of rice noodles, bean sprouts and green onions with thin slices of beef laid on top, all in a clear fragrant broth topped with chopped local vegetables and enhanced by a squirt of *nuoc mam*, fermented fish sauce (much more delicious than it sounds). As she walks back through the office with it, a mouth-watering smell envelops us. I eat it at my desk with my resident chopsticks while trying to field intermittent telephone calls. Later, certain pieces of correspondence will feature mysterious spots which I will of course be at a loss to explain.

At noon, I take off for our two-hour lunch break. The streets are jammed with traffic as the Vietnamese have a long lunch break and they are all going home. It takes me about ten minutes to traverse the few blocks, the prime holdup being at "confusion corner," the main crossroad where new policemen have been introduced into the melee to direct traffic – thus bringing everything to a virtual standstill. Once we clear this bottleneck, we are home free and I can be out at the pool in about two minutes. The maid has cleaned up last night's debris and prepared me fresh pineapple slices that will be welcomed after the broiling sun bath. The dogs are sound asleep on the cool tile floor and lurch out into the glaring sunlight, blinking and stretching. I jump into my bikini, grab a towel and radio and go out to the pool. The dogs follow me reluctantly and flop down under a table, changing positions frequently to find a cooler spot. I do the same at the edge of the pool, plunging in to cool off but careful not to get my long hair wet as I would never last the day in the office where I sit directly under an air conditioner.

It is approaching the rainy season so by one o'clock my agony has ended as the sky has become overcast and dark clouds are scudding ominously toward us. I take my steaming body back into the hooch to cool off under the shower and the dogs flop down again on the tile floor. As I dry off, the first drops of rain begin to fall on the tin roof and soon the dull roar blocks out even the radio music. Under this soothing sound, the dogs and I can't wait for our short nap on the waterbed; we all three lie flat on our backs and let the sound and cool air wave over our bodies. I awake abruptly at ten minutes to 2:00 as if a little alarm clock had gone off in my head, leap up and get dressed, now thoroughly refreshed. I gobble down several pieces of pineapple as I go out the door.

The office is quiet and I know the lunch hour here has also been as Colonel Wilson's phone rings in my home as well as at the office so that I can catch it on nights when the office is closed. The maid appears at my elbow with a steaming cup of coffee as I sit down at my desk. She will check frequently to be sure that it's hot – and that no bugs have fallen into it. I have become so completely Vietnamized that when I found a dead fly in my soup the other day I simply fished it out and continued eating, grateful it was only a fly and not a cockroach (where I do draw the line). She will also polish my shoes, sew hems in my dresses, go to the market for me or do any little chore I ask, considering all this to be a maid's job. This utterly floors Americans who back home have had to wash windows because their American maids considered this beneath them. In return, I buy candy for her children and bring back a little present for her after each R&R trip out of the country – we are allowed two-per year. She apparently considers this more than a fair exchange as the items I pick up in Hong Kong are of real use to her, high quality ones that cost ten times as much on the local market.

By now the rain is really coming down and I can barely see the cars parked six feet from the door. Gradually the trickle coming into the waiting room from under the front door becomes heavier. The maid comes out with her mops and bucket and fights to keep the water out of Colonel Wilson's office. Alas, water is now trickling down the stairs in the back hallway so we are now threatened on two fronts until one of our local workmen comes to the door lugging sand bags that he piles in the back corridor and against the front door, stopping the inward flow. The phones keep ringing, interrupting our labors as an amused and non-helpful Lieutenant sits placidly on the couch, feet up and marveling at our "Chinese fire drill" scene. The downpour soon passes, the floors are mopped and the office returns to normal.

The afternoon speeds by with little flurries of activity as we try to get the reports finished in time to be hand-carried out to the airport and then sent to Saigon on the regular evening flight. With twenty minutes to flight time we send a driver out with a last-minute envelope that he will hand to the "kicker". He is normally the guy who kicks cargo out the door of the C-130, but now is the guy who finally closes the door on the plane before it taxis out. He will in turn hand the packet to a designated passenger and our responsibility ends there. Occasionally we have a dum-dum who will hand a classified document to the kicker or else leave it on a desk or in a car or some other insecure place, so by now we have learned which couriers to avoid.

The front door opens and an oddly-dressed (part military, part civies) scruffy-looking young man comes in, all hair but a nice smile. I welcome him warmly (I enjoy the offbeat) and find that he is not a "hippy" but a respected reporter from a London newspaper. He is modest and charming and soon has Miss Hanh and me involved in some of the chores that are supposed to be handled by the PIO (Public Information Officer) but seldom are. I like him all the more because the army guys get so tight-jawed when dealing with guys like him, ones who like to wander around unsupervised. So far he says he has not had to fight for that right in the Delta, but he does sometimes get a lot of flack from some junior officers when he shows up at any of their clubs, especially if he has a lovely Vietnamese girl on his arm.

I get the lad on his way and will see him on several occasions later as he pops back by the office on his way to and from the various provinces. He always teases Miss Hanh about her being his personal secretary and she banters with him in her slangy English, fussing at him in a good-natured way. We don't mind doing extra things for people we like, but the constant demands from total strangers or lazy colleagues unwilling to take care of their own people drive us wild. We feel like we've become booking agents for Air America for about half the Delta as we assign priorities, coordinate schedules and try to sort out whose needs are legit and whose not.

We hear the chopper landing and we immediately start a series of phone calls to people waiting to see Colonel Wilson so that they will be available the moment he comes in. He strides through the front door looking tired and adds some names to the list of people to be called. The maid scurries in with a cup of hot coffee that I manage to get into Wilson's office before the first visitor closes the door. I hear him bellow proudly, "How do you like my new pictures?" We have just completed the hanging of about fifteen new photographs he has taken while on leave in Australia, Singapore, Bali, and other exotic climes. They have been mounted beautifully in Bangkok and now line the paneled walls, along with the numerous plaques presented to him during his long service in the US Army in war and peace. The pictures and plaques relieve some of the austerity of the brown walls, the steel desk and filing cabinet and a few arm chairs for visitors.

The pilot comes in for his next day's assignment and sits down to shoot the breeze with us. Today Colonel Wilson wanted to go into Kien Luong, a town that either was or is under VC control, depending on who is issuing the news release. Colonel Wilson indicated with his hand to drop down low and come in slow so they could do a visual recon. The pilot timidly submitted that he would suggest a "high overhead," i.e., an approach where you stay at your flying altitude until you are directly over the target then spiral down as rapidly as possible to minimize chances of taking ground fire.

Colonel Wilson looked up, irritated, and said: "I don't even remember the last time I was shot at." The pilot gulped and replied: "I do, sir, I do!" Now the pilot is grumbling that Colonel Wilson is after all sixty-three years old and not afraid of death because he has lived it all – but that he sees no reason for him to take this twenty-two year-old pilot, who has not yet lived it all, with him. The pilot, technically the aircraft's commander, has the authority to fly his machine as he thinks best and I call the pilot's bluff: Has he ever refused to fly as directed by Colonel Wilson? Well, no, not yet, he sheepishly admits, confirming my suspicion that his fear of Colonel Wilson is perhaps – at least at that moment – greater than his fear of death.

Although the Saigon plane has departed, Colonel Wilson

suddenly decides there are several urgent messages he must get to Saigon at once and dictates a few quick and cogent items that I rapidly type up and have back on his desk for signature, then off to the airport to get them to Saigon early next morning. We then sit down and review the schedule for the next few days, as he has decided we must have a dinner for a new visiting dignitary and his small staff, this one from the Australian Embassy in Saigon. He gives me the guest list and I will easily do the rest as these events are always held at the CORDS Club and the menu is always about the same. Colonel Wilson never entertains at home (meaning his Palm Springs super-hooch that he used to share with Vann) and never has cocktail parties, which he loathes (as do I).

I call the club manager and set up a dinner for eight with the "usual" – which will produce a relatively satisfactory dinner consisting of a seafood cocktail, prime ribs or a steak, a baked potato with sour cream, a local veggie, maybe a salad, an imported wine and either ice cream or an "American" apple pie for dessert. It is usually a hit, whether the visitors are American or Australian, as many have either been eating mess hall food or have gone local, eating Vietnamese delicacies (many of which leave you hungry later on). They are happy now to get a little 'real' food.

I will have to go over to the Club that day and check the table settings, add the place cards I have prepared, check to be sure they have used the good china, send a few wine glasses back to be polished, get the cursed plastic flowers off the center of the table and order fresh ones, and other minor adjustments that represent the total extent of my housekeeping, both domestic and official. The guards will be alerted to clear parking spaces for the VIP guests and to 'step up' security (whatever that means).

By now it is 1830 and the phones have virtually ceased to ring as 1800 represents the official close of business for Headquarters. The duty officer has already come in and been handed his little stack of assorted paraphernalia that he will need to get him through the night. We have left a thermos of hot coffee in the pantry for him but he does not have to stay awake unless there is big action somewhere. There is a cot back in the radio room where he can sleep and still monitor phones and radios. This duty is not particularly onerous, especially if you bring your Vietnamese girlfriend along – which some of the more daring and less conscientious types do. I have already begun to put away the classified material from the other offices and I putter around Wilson's desk in ever decreasing circles until he gives me the magic words: "OK, lock 'em up."

With that, I grab the In-Boxes and quickly shuffle through the stacks of paper on his desk to determine if we have overlooked anything classified he may have been reading and tucked away there. I toss the boxes into various drawers in the safe and begin to make my rounds of the offices, shutting off lights and air-conditioning, surveying desks for classified materials and sending coffee cups back to the pantry. I nip over to the duty officer's desk and pick up for Colonel Wilson a copy of *Stars and Stripes* if it has come in, and then recheck to be sure that the area is secured. I lock the two safes and initial their sign-out forms. Now I can give Colonel Wilson his newspaper to read as he departs and I can drive home.

As I drive out, the parking lot is already empty and the guards are waiting to roll shut the security gates for the night; this is only a recent innovation after the theft of two cars from the lot after duty hours. The sun is still bright and the crowded streets radiate the heat. Ben Xe Moi is now full of GIs and the *cyclo* drivers cluster around the doors of the more popular bars, hustling for the customers coming out. I must drive very slowly through this area, as there are already GIs weaving tipsily into the streets

– they have been at it steadily since 1600, when the town begins to fill up and the Army and Air bases to empty out. I navigate my car between and around them and they shout and wave and give me the V sign. Confusion Corner's traffic is moving at the usual pace and I slowly wend my way homeward into the setting sun.

At the gate of Palm Springs, the guard sees me approaching and flings the little STOP paddle out toward the traffic to allow me to turn right into the main gate. In any other right-hand drive territories, turning right would be no problem, but here Hondas and bicycles and everything else tend to pass you on the right as well as the left, further adding to the necessity for "swivel-heading" when driving. The guards at the gate salute me and motion for me to honk the horn; they love the blare of my Saab's Maserati air horn and always grin broadly when I blow it for them, signaling me to do it again. As I pull up beside my hooch, I can hear the dogs barking wildly; they too have heard my familiar horn and know I am coming. As I open the door, they rush toward me; we are all happy that I am home.

As the evening cools I sit out by the pool hoping to be allowed some solitude. Although this has not been a particularly busy day, I find that every day I need this few minutes to unwind after being so incessantly surrounded by people – and demands – during the workday. When the lights come on in the surrounding hooches, I return to my hooch to change. The smell of *nuoc mam* wafts through the air, momentarily startling me as it smells like a dead rat (that the dogs periodically try to present to me as a gift). But then I realize it is only a Vietnamese maid cooking dinner for one of the guys in the other three quadrants of my hooch.

My escort for my evening of dining out is a delightfully cynical young captain who used to work in the front office but has finally fulfilled his wish to get back to "the war"; he has the jeep motor running so I hop in and we zoom off. I like riding in open jeeps, despite the added precautions necessary such as protecting watches, glasses and pocketbooks with every hand. You feel like you are really part of the traffic flow. Tonight we go to our favorite restaurant, 'Olga's'. The young Vietnamese waiters all know us, but their ranks are now depleted by the latest VN draft call for seventeen-through-forty-three-year-olds.

The Chinese owner always bows as we file past him to go to the reserved upper floor. He knows that at the rate of the drawdown of troops in Can Tho, we may soon be his only customers, as the Vietnamese (other than the bar girls) are seldom seen eating here. I assume it has not always been an American hang-out and even we may be forced to visit it less frequently when all our offices are transferred out to the Can Tho airfield next year. Already the restaurant clientele is down steeply from its usual trade and tonight there are only two GIs and their Vietnamese girlfriends, but perhaps we are a little early tonight.

The waiters bring us hot washcloths lightly scented with "Mr. Clean", handing them to us with tongs, and we wipe our hands while the men scrub down their faces and sometimes whole heads, then make fake swipes under their armpits for humor. Thus refreshed, we are ready to study the long menu. We are familiar with it by now as we have a duplicate copy on which we strike off each item that we have ordered. By now, we are over fifty percent through the menu and have resolved never to disband this informal 'gourmand club' until we have sampled every item, with the possible exception of the hamburger with French fries, which would be an insult to the extensive French, Chinese and even American cuisine offerings.

Having never seen a cow in Vietnam (or anywhere in "the tropics" for that matter), I have always felt that ordering beef is a mistake since it was probably either water buffalo or, in Vietnam during this war, probably something 'requisitioned' from the US

Military through the back door. Indeed, we had discovered that was indeed Olga's source of supply (but this is Vietnam, and we did not ask further), so here the beef was just fine. In fact, last week, I ordered Tournedos with Sauce Bearnaise; it was absolutely delicious and the price was right: 850 Piaster – in a country where 425 Piaster equals US$1.00.) We drink a steady supply of "boppety-bops" (GI slang for the good local "33" or *ba muoi ba* beer) and Vietnamese limed iced tea served in gigantic glasses as we proceed with the business of eating and swapping lies that consumes a good hour.

By half an hour before curfew the restaurant is virtually empty, the GIs by then having gone to the bordellos and bars – only, to add to the confusion since the declaration of martial law closed all the bars they are now called "restaurants". But everyone knows the difference between restaurants and "restaurants", if only by the appearance of the waitresses. In the latter, when a red light goes on indicating Vietnamese police are in the area, the proprietor shoos the girls out the back door and drags out some dishes – and perhaps a bit of food for good measure.

The large cluster of *cyclos* around the door indicates that the "Hollywood" is still doing good business next door, despite the fact that they no longer have their ear-splitting acid rock band that used to make dining at Olga's a test for the nerves. I wonder if Big Lucy is still there, the brassy "star" who always greets me with a big hug and a "you my friend!" She was quite the hit at the last party I gave and I admire her forthrightness and businesslike approach; I hope she is surviving the hard times of this current drawdown plus the post- martial law slowdown.

We wave off the *cyclo* drivers and raise our hands over our heads to avoid the grasp of a gaggle of children, ages five through about ten, who cluster around us, plucking at our clothing (and watches, if they could reach them). They are not to be

taken lightly, as they managed to relieve three girls of two watches and a pair of glasses in broad daylight when we once long ago
emerged from Olga's without a male escort. Tonight they keep a
little more distance but still block our path, begging for money
or cigarettes or anything else we might have. It is said that the
softhearted and overly-generous GIs have turned the Vietnamese children into proficient beggars, and I am afraid there is more
than a little truth in that.

We walk past the CORDS Hotel to the parking reserved for
our headquarters and military vehicles and retrieve our jeeps,
the guard signs us out, noting license numbers and time of de-
partures as we drive through the gate. For almost a year now,
we have not been allowed to park on the streets. This causes a
bit of a hardship in Can Tho, but nothing like it does in Saigon,
where many official Americans are now obliged to park far from
their apartments every night. Here there is usually a parking lot
within a block of where we want to go, since there are so few
places we want to go, and I get preferential treatment in getting
parking spaces in them, maybe because I am known to be "from
Headquarters" – or maybe just because I'm a friendly female
who speaks 'Pidgin' Vietnamese to them (oh yes, and those cigarettes).

We drive along slowly behind a *cyclo* containing a GI sitting
bolt upright but swaying slightly. Suddenly he leans over the
side and neatly barfs, returning at once to his bolt upright position. The episode reduces us to giggles which last all the way
back to Palm Springs, where the gates are now locked. The guard
peeps through the eye slot and then raises the "Apache bar" and
opens the gate, swinging both sides wide to let in the jeep. I hop
out as my escort completes the circle to get out the gate before it
closes again.

The compound is quiet now when I walk the dogs. All the

lights have been turned off in the pool area which means that the skinny dippers will soon be coming out for their evening romp. We skirt the pool, making lots of noise so that the late bathers will know that we are here and are not to emerge like Venus from the half shell, as they did one night when Vann and the Secretary of Agriculture were skirting the pool. He said he and the Secretary pointedly ignored the nude pair because not seeing them called for no comment.

We continue our walk along the back of the hooches, past the generator house and the water filtration plant where the water tender sleeps beside his machinery, his straw pallet on a wooden platform under the overhanging roof with a voluminous mosquito net enveloping his cozy nest. He lives most of his life there, eating at the soup stand across the street or brewing tea on his little Sterno cooker; he may have a family someplace to whom he writes (if he can) or sends money, or he may have no one but himself. His wants are simple and his life simple but here he has companionship with the guards, technicians, compound's maid and others who come in daily. He always tries to get my dogs to come to him but they are uniformly distrustful of the Vietnamese – something I certainly never taught them – and will never respond to his overtures, but he does not take it personally and continues to be friendly to them and me.

The dogs and I skirt the holding tanks, sludgy and dirty-looking, and climb over the ammo box that is used as a step, squeezing past the oil drums filled with earth over near the compound wall that serve as our emergency mortar shelter (but I'll take my chances in my own bed, thank you), then complete the circle along the narrow passageway which runs between the laundry room and the hooches and this brings us once again to my door.

In the street, traffic is now thinning out and the National Police and PSDF (People's Self Defense Force) are setting up a checkpoint to apprehend deserters, draft-dodgers and Honda-riding cowboys, so I know the night will be punctuated by rifle fire as they fire over the heads (hopefully) of the young men flee-ing on Hondas. I often wonder in passing where all those bullets finally land. (I am a fatalist, luckily, as the thin wooden walls and tin roof of my hooch would otherwise give me very little peace of mind.) Before I even take off my shoes I turn on the ten o'clock news roundup, which is only a slight variation on the morning's offerings. I will stay awake for the news until almost midnight. It's amazing how very late midnight seems in a world where the curfew starts at nine-thirty in the evening.

I think of other happier and busier days when we could stay out until midnight and I was dating a dashing Air Force Major. As he had now left, I was casually dating a General (definitely moving up through the ranks!). That relationship also was grad-ually becoming more intense – as always in war, it seems – but because of his high profile, it was far more discrete (the friend-ship was also clearly a deep one, however, and lingered on for a long time after I returned to the US).

My life actually now was not that different: work, swimming, dogs, bridge, poolside chats and parties, movies at the CORDS Hotel, trips by auto (mine or others') through the countryside and to the shore (now discontinued due to the current securi-ty situation), and of course flying (Space-A) up to Saigon some weekends to visit friends and a few more sophisticated locales than Can Tho offered, such as the Continental Hotel.

I would sometimes sit there on the "Continental Shelf' out-door terrace with a fellow CORDS gal, the beautiful tall and blonde Lily. My pilot used to call it "Trolling with Lily", and I thought that would make a great title for a book about Round Eyes in Vietnam. We would have no more than sat down than the table would be surrounded by men jockeying for position –

officers, pilots, even the occasional Frenchman left over from the old rubber plantations upcountry, now too dangerous to oversee, or even visit.

Then came the small bouquets of jasmine, drinks, requests to sit down with us, and all sort of approaches. After the usual questions – where we were from, what we were doing here, etc. – a lively and competitive conversation would ensue. But Lily had her love elsewhere, as did I, so none of their ploys – although some quite charming and clever – succeeded. Anyhow, it was fun being the center of so much male attention. What female wouldn't love that?

Lily was obviously the most beautiful blonde most of them had seen in the past year (or length of their tour). Not only did she not seem to know it, but was as friendly and nice as you will ever find in such a fine creature. Down in the Delta, our Lily also caused a sensation wherever she went, both with Americans and with the Vietnamese officers and officials. They would often ask to be photographed individually at her side, they beaming as she towered over them. (I suspect later the photo would be presented to admiring colleagues as one of the men's conquests, or perhaps his mistress.)

I suppose it is the war combined with the lack of stabilizing influences in a very chaotic society that makes romances bloom so rapidly in Vietnam. Either partner will leave at the end of a tour or sometimes on rather short notice, and the fact that the liaison will be terminated in the foreseeable future adds a special intensity to relationships. So far from home, we tend to create our own little monogamous nests. Few of us have any illusions about the permanence of the liaisons, but the separation from families and isolation from "The World" leads us to conclude that even a few months of shared happiness is worth the inevitable price of future heartaches.

As I lie there alone in my hooch feeling rather sorry for my-self, I watch the geckos skitter across the ceiling. The ones near the light are so full of bugs that they look like little ping pong balls with feet and tails as they sluggishly move around the lamp; I could swear I see one burp as he plods along. The sounds of *Nielsson Schmielson* accompany the pattern of big drops of rain that begin to fall on the roof; if we have a typical monsoon rain-storm, it will soon entirely drown out the music. But now the soothing sound makes me drowsy and I rouse the dogs and chiv-vy them into their dog houses under the kitchen table. I crawl back into bed and fall asleep to the sound of the now-drumming rain.

The ringing of a phone at my right ear awakens me out of my deep sleep. As I am a sound sleeper, it takes me a moment to real-ize where I am and that it is the office phone that has ended my slumber. I grope for the light and glance at the clock: it is 3:00am. The faint voice of our PSA (Province Senior Advisor) greets me from somewhere in the static of the telephone system.

Is Colonel Wilson there? I explain patiently that Colonel Wil-son's phone also rings in my home as well as the office and that he is a very heavy sleeper and seldom hears the phone at night after 9:30. If it is truly important, I can always go over and beat on the window by his bed in the hopes of waking him up. The PSA informs me there is a very serious fire raging in the province and that they need help of some kind – what kind, he is just not sure. I point out that Colonel Wilson is hardly in a position to help them, since we have neither fire trucks nor Pedros (foam-carrying choppers), so do we really want to notify Colonel Wil-son? I am actually not being as officious as I sound; I just know from past experience that Colonel Wilson does not want to be notified of anything in the middle of the night unless he can do something about it or if it involves the death or a serious threat to any of our US advisors assigned there.

Once before, I had finally awakened Colonel Wilson after standing outside his window for what seemed like ages, alternately pounding and shouting – much to the amusement of the guards who patrolled by. When I then informed Colonel Wilson that five Americans were missing somewhere in a remote area of a province, he said, "Well, they couldn't be ours, we don't have that many men in the area, so don't worry about it." I accordingly didn't, and it turned out that he was right as usual. They were five Navy advisors who had strayed into the wrong area but emerged – undoubtedly shaken – the next day, safe after a false move that could have gone far worse for them.

Since I am unable to dissuade this PSA, who is noted anyway for his total inability to make a decision for himself, I give up and promise to hang up and let the phone ring until Colonel Wilson answers it. As I try to get back to sleep, ten or fifteen minutes later it begins to ring again and this time I let it ring. After about fifty rings it stops so I know that either Colonel Wilson got it himself or they gave up – I could not care less at this stage. I finally drift off to sleep again and feel that I've not been asleep more than a few minutes (actually it was half hour by the clock) when the damn thing starts ringing anew.

I pick it up with considerable irritation and, sure enough, it is our PSA again. Would I tell Colonel Wilson that the fire was not as serious as he thought, that it is now under control and Colonel Wilson need not send the chopper that he has ordered – and, oh yes, would I cancel that chopper, too, please? I am ready to scream into the phone, "I told you so, you nitwit!" when I hear Colonel Wilson once again pick up the extension, so I say sweetly, "I think Colonel Wilson is on the phone now, so why don't you just tell him all this?"

I know the PSA would rather pass the buck to me than have to admit he panicked prematurely and now has to request a recall of a chopper that must have been difficult to get to begin with. My irritation is partly at being awakened because of someone else's inability to take responsibility, but mostly because my boss should not be troubled by such matters when that is what we have PSA's in the province for. This particular PSA gets double my salary and yet Miss Hanh and I frequently have to make his decisions for him when he calls – almost daily– with his "Do you think I should …?" or "Would Colonel Wilson want me to…?"

Miss Hanh and I are used to hearing his problems and complaints by now and we usually listen with resignation, weigh the factors and then make our own recommendation as to what he should do. It never seems to strike him as inappropriate that an American and a Vietnamese secretary should be advising him on what course of action to take. In fact, he always seems to hang up considerably relieved to have been spared the responsibility of the decision. We despair.

It is now after 0400 and still raining; I am glad I did not have to go out in my raincoat to wake my boss. If the phone does not ring again, I can get about two more hours of sleep before facing another Day of Duty in the Delta.

12

A Slow Road Back to Saigon

After Colonel Wilson's death I had lost my job and having worked with two of the most effective and charismatic leaders in Vietnam, I was not enthusiastic about seeking yet another boss, inevitably a lesser light. I did, however, want to see how it was all going to turn out in Vietnam; now that the US troops had been drawn down, the country's fate was up to the ARVN and a now-drastically reduced contingent of US advisors. When I was offered a short interim assignment with USAID in serene and lovely Laos, I accepted.

My first worry on being given this TDY (temporary duty) assignment was about transporting my two young dachshunds there by plane. On arriving at the airport with baggage, dogs and a dog crate (which I really did not want to stuff them into), I sauntered up to the Air America pilot smoking his last cigarette at the foot of the boarding stairs and had a little chat with him. Luckily for me, he happened to be a dog lover and of course he allowed me to take the pups aboard. I could have kissed him (and possibly did). So instead of being down in the hold with some dirty and possibly dangerous baggage, like ammo, the dogs were in the cabin with me under a blanket in my lap. Lulled by the hum of the propellers, we slept the sleep of the innocent.

My office in Vientiane turned out to be in a remote corner of the USAID headquarters compound. I was usually the sole occupant, as my boss and the rest of the small staff were, presumably, out in the field. I did wonder, however, what they were doing as all I ever had in the way of work was to type one or two short and boring reports. I must have been still numb from the sudden change in fortune, as most of my three-month Laos stint is now a total blank. I do remember clearly, however, that with virtually no work to do, it was deadly dull, especially for someone who thrives on excitement.

The capital itself was a rather sleepy tropical outpost, heavily French-influenced and thus at least with great local restaurants left over from their tenure there. It also had a fairly small American presence, an Embassy and USAID being the major contributors. We officials had two residential compounds, Silver City downtown and KM-6, located, as you would expect, six kilometers out of town. I and my dachsies were housed in a small villa with luxuriant planting and an efficient local housekeeper who turned out to be a divine cook – it must have been those French again! Life could have been a pleasant colonial one but with no visible war, no friends there and nothing happening in the office, it was Dullsville. I thanked the gods daily for my dogs and my books; otherwise I think I would have gone bananas.

I did get something unexpected out of it: a trip up to Luang Prabang, the former kingly capital perched on a hill overlooking a meandering river. It is one of the most magical places I have ever been. Saffron-robed monks bearing begging bowls wandered through the streets. There were only a few guest houses, no hotels and no tourists. There was a war going on in Laos but it was hardly noticeable up there. The evenings were quiet, the only sound the tinkling of hundreds of tiny bells that hung beneath the eaves of the village's many temples. I now know how lucky I was to get there before the world was to discover this little jewel and overrun it.

I had one more memorable moment, my first – and only – Palace Coup. While out in the garden of my villa one morning, I heard, somewhere in the distance, a muffled explosion. Then I saw a small plane circling over the city. A bomb did cross my mind but in such a peaceful setting, I dismissed that idea. Minutes later, the phone rang. It was the USAID duty officer telling me not to come to the office as a coup was at that moment taking place at the palace and they didn't know how it would all turn out.

The palace was about four miles from me and I stayed in the garden staring up at the sky, but the plane never returned. After waiting a while with nothing happening, I decided to go into town and see what was going on. I'd been told not to come to work – but not to stay out of town. Before I could leave, however, another call came telling me to report to work after all. The coup was over, the rebels had lost, and possibly were shot right on the spot – but this being a peaceable kingdom, perhaps not. Life anyway was back to normal. This gentle country it was probably just your traditional coup.

I followed daily the news out of Vietnam to see what was happening in Can Tho and with my friends. The American troops had been drawing down steadily for some time and by late August, most were gone. Negotiations in France portended the setting up of American consulates in CORDS' old headquarters locations, so this meant there would soon be an American Consulate in Can Tho.

In 1973, the eagerly-awaited call finally came. I was to be the secretary to the new Consul in Can Tho. I would soon be back in my old hooch at Palm Springs and in our old office building, alas now without Vann and his helicopter on the roof. We all had liked being in an office right in the front and center of the building, where all the action took place, just as Vann had also chosen it for ease of exiting in his usual sprint out the front door to his chopper.

But now with Vann, Colonel Wilson, and Frenchy all gone, it would not be the same. Now the Consul's and my offices were more serenely located on the second floor at the rear of our old building, formerly *terra incognita* to me. I would be back and in my old world but now one sadly diminished, no chopper taking off over our heads, no shouting into field telephones, and no more excitement, I feared.

I had a great deal of leave saved up and used some of it to cover the assignment gap. Serving in Vietnam not only got us a paid trip each year to the US, but we could also use local leave to go to the R&R sites set up by the military for the troops to get away from the war for a week or two. Courtesy of Uncle Sam, I had visited all the surrounding Asian countries except China, and that would come later. I even got as far afield as Australia, the troops' favorite R&R site because, it was reliably reported, "Australian girls can't say No".

As a World War II buff, I utilized one R&R opportunity to go to the Philippines to visit the sad remnants of Corregidor. I stood in the colossal ruins of Topside, the battered stone barracks atop the hill, and walked through the island's empty, echoing Malinta Tunnel. From there, the Japanese had sent those who survived its bombardment on the notorious Bataan Death March that killed so many American POWs. The island's atmosphere hung heavy with its heartbreaking history where so many had died so early in the long Pacific War. Now everything was overgrown, lush and peaceful but I felt I was walking on sacred ground, although the graves of most who fought here lay far away or unmarked.

On R&R flights, if we were not officially authorized, there were always a few empty seats left over from guys who could not get down country in time to make the flight. Once when I was up in Saigon for a week on a TDY, I came across two EMs who had just missed their R&R flight. They were a picture of dejection, two Southern boys just down from some heavy fighting up in I Corps, hapless and helpless. They deserved better, so I took pity on them and set them up for a local R&R: First I gave them a bottle of bourbon and then I directed them to a famous local café that served huge Southern-style breakfasts (AKA 'Heart-Attack-on-a-Plate').

I used to love to take or send unsuspecting out-of-towners there, always touting that Southern specialty. What I did not mention to them was that all the waitresses were both topless and bottomless, although semi-modestly covered below by pretty little aprons. It was fun to watch the visitors' faces when it suddenly dawned on them that this just might not be your standard American diner after all.

At the end of the week, the boys came by to thank me. As I anticipated, in the café they had both met the Loves of Their Lives and had spent almost the entire week shacked up in some local hotel. They looked hung-over and exhausted – and were grinning from ear to ear. In retrospect, I think that in all my years in Vietnam that was probably the greatest service that I ever rendered anyone.

Back at my new job in Can Tho, I learned that as part of the contingent asked to cover the observance of the Paris Peace Accords, a batch of some fifteen FSOs (Foreign Service Officers) would arrive in Can Tho in January of 1973. They were called Vice-Consuls. As some of them had previously held the title of Consul, their new title caused great unhappiness, as they now felt themselves going backward. The Consul in charge had said that he wanted a clear distinction between the head of the mission – i.e., himself – and everyone else, so Vice-Consuls they remained, although there was a lot of grumbling about it before they got down to work.

These FSOs had served previous tours in Vietnam and all could speak Vietnamese. Now they were to fan out to all the provinces in the four corps to report on what they saw and heard. Their long and detailed reports started pouring in and kept me busy for weeks on end. These officers were the *crème de la crème* of the Foreign Service's Vietnam contingent and later most went on to outstanding careers in the Service or in the private sector.

They included the bright and cynical young officer, Lacy Wright, with whom I had served earlier in Can Tho. After that and a tour in London, Lacy had returned to Vietnam and stayed on to the end. During the dangerous final days in Saigon, the Ambassador put him in charge of evacuating the Vietnamese relatives of Americans, a number of whom by then had married into Vietnamese families. For ten days, Lacy operated safe houses from which evacuees were spirited to the airport by American drivers from our embassy. On the last day, he drove through the streets picking up designated Vietnamese evacuees wherever he could find them. That night, he was lifted off the roof of the Embassy. He remains to this day my friend, and one of the funniest guys alive. In fact, friends from my Vietnamese tours remain some of my closest; shared danger and experiences forge strong and enduring bonds.

As the fifteen reporting officers gradually finished their assignments and departed, the work level dropped down to the predictable – and sometimes boring. By now being in the field had lost its zing for me. I did get a nice award for my service there (although it was not nearly so treasured as the medal that John Paul Vann had proudly pinned on me a few years earlier).

I felt rather out of the loop in Can Tho, as Saigon now seemed to be where things were happening – or going to. I was ripe for a new assignment when a tempting offer came in: to be seconded to USIS (the US Information Service) to work for their top man in Saigon. In the fall of 1973, I moved my modest household to my new digs in the capital. They proved to be a considerable step up from the hooches that had been my homes for most of my seven years in Vietnam.

I now had a two-bedroom flat in a USIS-leased apartment building just off Cong Ly, the main road between downtown Saigon and the airport and the one I had driven down that first day I had arrived in Saigon. It was in a pre-war building with generous-sized rooms, high ceilings and lazy ceiling fans, cool tiled floors, and a long balcony along the entire front of the apartment.

My first bit of homesteading was to cut a doggie door through one of the double doors leading from the living room to the balcony. I then filled the balcony with bowls of goldfish, exotic tropical plants and bird cages with singing birds. My favorites were a pair of turtle doves. I gave them their freedom on the day I finally left Vietnam; they flew to the roof of the villa in front of me, sat a long time looking back at their old home, and then flew off to a new life.

I next hired an amah to take care of me and my menagerie. Her name was Zhao – which I thought sounded like stepping on a cat's tail – and she was a Chinese-Vietnamese. The name could have tipped me, off but I did not then know that it was a typically Chinese name. The Chinese-Vietnamese controlled most of the lucrative businesses in Vietnam. She turned out to be a better cook than even my Lao one, so again I was blessed by the gods – who perhaps take pity on those who cannot cook.

The kitchen was large with a whole wall full of cabinets, all with locks. Vietnamese housewives carry with them at all times huge rings of keys because they keep all food and supplies locked up, doling them out to the cook and staff as needed, and then re-locking away the remainder. I did not lock up anything and, for the first time in Vietnam, I did not see my things – everything from hair spray to diamond ear studs – disappear at a steady rate, or indeed at all.

Zhao was not only honest but also extremely thrifty and for pennies a day she turned out delicious meals for me, both Vietnamese and Chinese. She also saved everything. Once I mistakenly combined two small bags of bird seed for my flock with the sesame seeds she had bought for her cooking. I told her to just toss them all and we would start over. But later I came into the kitchen and found her sitting on the floor with a white cloth spread out beside her and a heap of seeds in the middle. One by one she was separating the seeds into two separate little piles – whose total worth was probably the equivalent of five US cents.

The servants' rear entrance to the kitchen was via a circular staircase that turned out to be ideal for stringing my hammock as it was on the shady side of the building. The kitchen was of course also tiled and that kept its floor cool. I only discovered that my amah slept there when one night instead of ringing the call bell, I went to get some ice tea out of the fridge. On the floor there lay Zhao on her back on a straw mat with a dog on either side of her, all three sleeping soundly under the revolving ceiling fan. I wish I had photographed it.

Thanks to my two dachshunds, I also got to renew a few old friendships with members of our Embassy staff in Saigon. I became friends with Eva, the Ambassador's secretary who was also a dachshund owner; she and her foreign correspondent boyfriend, later husband, owned six dachshunds between them. We often shared critical information about veterinary services and of course traded the inevitable dog stories – and we remain friends to this day.

The USIS in Saigon had turned a mansard-roofed French villa

into a workable and rather nifty office building. Our "Front Office" was in what had probably been the master bedroom suite and the former large garden was now paved over to serve as a parking lot. The boss was a hard-charger, very handsome and exceptionally vain with a brand-new blonde trophy wife, a former foreign correspondent. She was as good-looking as he was and they made a striking couple but I think she led him a merry chase; I heard that they later divorced. Since I had just come from the field where there was still a war on and things were a bit more basic, my boss's keen concern for his creature comforts was sometimes trying for me and the rest of his small staff. I think one example says it all.

My job unfortunately turned out to be mostly just many months of routine boredom; the only saving graces was that the office was in the center of the city and I was working for an interesting person, albeit an 'unguided missile' – the USIS director. At least running his personal errands got me out of the office quite a bit and I finally learned to appreciate a Saigon that I had seen only briefly some six years earlier.

My boss loved cottage cheese. This was not always available in the Army's commissary so we spent a lot of our time all over Saigon trying to track down this delicacy for him. One day he sent me out to try again; I had failed him on the last few attempts, so the matter was getting critical. Once more I drove over to the commissary only to find that its Vietnamese employees were staging a sit-down strike over some grievance and I could not drive through the main entrance because Vietnamese men and women were sitting in a row across it facing outward, completely blocking access.

I parked my car outside the gate and decided I could probably slip by them by walking in. About to head for the commissary, I saw a large American car coming very slowly out, driven by an American woman (wives were by then allowed to live in Saigon). She stopped, then slowly inched forward until the car's bumper was against the back of the necks of the Vietnamese sitting in the roadway. One of the fellow strikers standing on the side got angry, walked over to the car and pounded on the hood. At that point the irate – or perhaps frightened – woman floored it.

She shot through the gate and ran over several Vietnamese – and then all hell broke loose. People started screaming and running toward the car and the fallen Vietnamese. The Vietnamese gate guards pulled out their guns and starting firing indiscriminately. I ducked down behind my car just in time to see a Vietnamese man a few yards from me clutch at his chest. Just as in the movies, a red stain started spreading on his white shirt front as he slowly crumpled to the ground. Other Vietnamese rushed over to him, there were more shots, more screams, shouts, wailing, utter chaos. I stayed hunkered down there with a clear sight line and watched it all unravel, as if in slow motion, before me.

The White Mice and our Security guys finally arrived on the scene and started trying to take control and sort it all out. One of the Americans spotted me by my car and asked if I had seen it all. I had, and I turned out to be one of the few uninvolved eyewitnesses to the entire incident, from its start to its tragic finish; I thus had to go immediately down to Security headquarters to give a statement. I asked the Security officer to call my office and tell my boss why I would be late, then I sat down and wrote a long testimony of what had happened. I waited until it was typed up, signed it, and finally was allowed to return to my office. Some four hours had elapsed since I had left on my critical errand and I was sweaty, disheveled and utterly drained by all I had seen and been through.

Back in the office, I breathlessly started telling my boss all that I had seen, the dead bodies, the man getting shot, the whole horrible scene. After a few moments he stopped me in my tracks with a question: "But did you get my cottage cheese?" Alas, I had not.

The driver, as I recall, was whisked out of the country before nightfall.

My friend Eva was one of the Foreign Service's highest-ranking secretaries and she was a whiz. I was told that once she was typing an important document when there was a gigantic, earth-shaking explosion near our old Embassy. She rose a few inches off her chair as things crashed and banged around her and then descended again without looking up or missing a typewriter stroke. She had survived the 1965 bombing of the Embassy that killed several Americans and many Vietnamese, so I guess she was used to explosions.

We sometimes ate at a restaurant near the old Embassy (this was not the new replacement one from which she and the Ambassador were helicoptered off the roof on the last day). The restaurant was known for its good food and fast service and was obviously not Vietnamese – they liked to enjoy their food in a more leisurely fashion. It was, of course, Chinese. One could eat well and fast there so it was popular with the Embassy's busy staff. We also often met at the same parties and I got to know her well. And her home in the Washington area later served as my "second home" during my many trips to the US.

It was thanks to Eva that I got onto the roster for a flight to Nepal. We had a rare Foreign Service situation where two Ambassadors were married to each other. Ambassador Bunker's wife, Carol Laise, was the Ambassador to Nepal, and he periodically flew on a government plane to consult with her. Since there was usually only the Ambassador, his aide and his secretary aboard, there were always places left over for strap-hangers. I was thus fortunate to get to see Kathmandu in the days before it too was hit by progress and became a Mecca for backpackers. It was then a magical kingdom, closed to the outside world and inhabited by a gentle people who were still living in an earlier century.

I was living a pleasant but rather aimless "colonial" life, swimming at the *Cercle Sportif*, trips out every few months to nearby countries, high pay and not really much work to do. I missed the excitement that working for Vann and Wilson had always provided, challenging us all and keeping us busy. I also now felt the situation was never going to change in Vietnam; the war seemed to have stalemated and nothing much was ever going to happen here. (I also predicted, much later in East Berlin, that The Wall would never fall in my lifetime. So much for *my* political sophistication.)

My contract with USIS was running down and I did not want to renew it. I realized it was high time to depart Vietnam and get back to a more regular way of life. My best and beloved bosses had died, most of my friends had left, and the time had obviously come to return to my home country and resume my former life there, in Washington, in Virginia, or wherever.

In late 1974, with reluctance but resignation, I finally ended my seven years in that lovely and tortured country and flew to San Francisco, picked up my dogs (shipped earlier to a dog-loving friend there), and returned to 'Real Life' to become re-Americanized. I was now 43 years old and during the trip I reflected on what I had done and what I had yet to do in life. I was antsy to get back to work, so I then flew home to Virginia. I took my combat pay and moved to Washington, D.C.

I rejoined the State Department's Foreign Service and moved into a row house in Georgetown and could walk to work each morning. I worked for six months in its Ops Center that maintains 24-hour contact with all Foreign Service posts worldwide.

It was fitting, perhaps, that I was on night duty there the day that Vietnam fell. I pulled the 'shutting down' message off the telex machine and I handed it the Ops Officer. He glanced at it and said simply, "It's over."

The room suddenly fell silent and I know that some of us had tears in our eyes.

13

Vietnam 30 Years Later

In 2004 I DECIDED that I wanted to visit Vietnam again to see if anything was left of the places I remembered from my wartime years there. Joined by a Hong Kong friend, we flew down to Saigon, then extended our trip up to the hill station of Dalat – which I had last visited some 35 years ago – and then to Hanoi, which I definitely had not. The last time I had been in Vietnam it was enemy territory. (But you would be surprised at the number of clueless Americans who ask me if I had – and I say 'well. only if I were a POW!" – which always startles them.)

This later trip yielded some mixed impressions and some good memories, and revalidated for me what I remembered: what a lovely country Vietnam is and how handsome its people are.

My first jolt of recognition came when we landed at Tan Son Nhut Airport, where I had first landed some forty years earlier. Its once small and shabby arrivals hall was greatly improved (but not yet world class). But the revetments were still there, left over from a time when they protected planes from rocket and mortar attacks. Now they were simply a convenient place to store the smaller planes. Nothing else looked familiar at the airport, but when we started our drive into town, it all came back to me. Not the buildings, as they were much modified, but they still evoked the "feeling" of the place.

It started with the swarm of undisciplined traffic, the sounds and smells and chaos of the traffic – now mostly motor bikes instead of jeeps, bicycles and *cyclos*. It all brought the old Saigon back to me. The slim women drivers still wore their traditional native dress (the *ao dai*) and white gloves, and covered their faces with veils or scarves to protect them from the sun; the young men still wove insouciantly in and out of traffic at high speed. Then there were the families all ingeniously wedged into a tight configuration using every available inch of the motorbike – two small children between the legs of the driver, a mother with babe in arms sitting behind him, and extra children precariously perched on the luggage rack at the rear. They did not even look crowded, all sitting there serenely as they putt-putted along in a cloud of smog. I looked for the familiar *cyclos*, but in these sub-urbs beyond the airport, they would have been overwhelmed (and stifled) by the hoards of exhaust-spewing motor bikes that flowed around our taxi like schools of minnows; I was to find the ubiquitous *cyclos* later, as usual, in the city center, often clustered near the hotels and bars.

Unlike Shanghai's streets, where cars get two lanes each and bicycles and motorbikes must make do with one narrow one, in Vietnam the number of motorbikes was so great that only one lane was allotted to cars and only two to motorbikes – and even that was not enough. Motorbikes also chose the option of con-sidering themselves either pedestrians or vehicles, depending on which had the go-ahead, and they wove in and out between the cars with the same total disregard for the rules of the road as in China. Surprisingly, however, the whole time we were there we did not see a single accident involving a motorbike. Despite the critical mass, they seamlessly melded into the traffic flow from all angles and without a backward or sideward glance – and, miraculously, it worked.

The drive to our hotel was a short one, as it was a former BOQ (bachelor officers' quarters) on the main road leading into town. Although any resemblance had been more or less obliterated in renovations, the location was just as I remembered. The manager told us that first the North Vietnamese had moved in, then the Russians, then the Vietnamese again, each successively doing more damage. By the time the hotel's investor – an early-arriving and astute Japanese – had bought the building, it was a hollow shell, stripped of all wood and even the metal window frames. But purchasing an intact shell had put him ahead of those hoteliers who had to build from the ground up, so the hotel was one of the first new five-star ones to open in the city and was now part of the Omni Hotel chain.

Once one of the jewels of France's Indo-Chinese colonies, Saigon, with its population now doubled, was too overbuilt, congested and smog-ridden to any longer rank as a beautiful city. There were still scattered small islands of beauty and charm, an old villa here, an elegant old hotel or government building there, some broad boulevards and spacious parks, but one could not characterize it as beautiful. But then, it had not been beautiful during the war either.

For me, this was a trip back down memory's corridor. Our first stop in my search for my past was in the old city center near the opera house, now garishly renovated. It was the old French hotel nearby, the Continental, that I used to sit on its street-side terrace, the Continental Shelf, and drink a citron pressé. Now the lovely old hotel was sadly modernized, its old shutters and overhanging roof gone, another storey added atop it and its open terrace walled and glassed in, separating it from contact with the street and all its lively activity (maybe that was the idea?).

The same applied to my first home in Saigon, the nearby Oscar Hotel, where I had once briefly shared a large front suite. In the Oscar, however, renovations had improved the ambience from that of a utilitarian wartime BOQ to a tourist hotel, replete with a doorman and chandeliers in its marble lobby. Not a thing was recognizable or familiar.

This was not true of our third stop, the roof of the Rex Hotel. If there is one icon that almost every American military man in the Saigon area remembers, it is the top of the Rex, then the largest and most diversely-equipped of the downtown BOQs. Besides the usual bar, restaurant and roof garden, it also had souvenir shops, tailors, massage parlors and everything an eager soldier could possibly desire – if not inside, then just outside the front door. It was on the roof that we sometimes spent the evenings with our dates watching the rocket and mortar attacks taking place just across the river. Sipping cheap beer and dollar hard drinks – no wonder alcohol consumption in Vietnam was endemic – we sat and watched with cool detachment the panoply of war. When I started serving in the field a few months later I would rapidly lose that cool detachment.

The view from the rooftop terrace, all now tarted up for the tourists, was spoiled by intervening high-rises that blocked out the opposite river bank, and the drinks were a great deal more expensive. We strolled the nearby streets, now lined with sophisticated boutiques and restaurants. Gaggles of tourists were doing the purchasing, not the carousing military of the earlier era. Needless to say, downtown Saigon no longer had the vibrancy it once had, but it was now much more tidy.

A trip to the old Chinese market hall in Cholon I found still chaotic. The mellow old colonial-era building was still a beehive of buying and selling, shouting and shoving. Merchandise still spilled out onto the passageways, delivery men pushed carts through throngs of shoppers, banging legs and running over toes. It was the same frenetic market that I so well remembered. not only the open produce and meat sections but also the general-merchandise niches that still supplied simple mixed-use items around the fringes.

It had been steamy, spicy, chaotic, and very Chinese. Now. there was not a single Chinese sign visible, indicating that they had long ago been assimilated, displaced or expelled by the Vietnamese government. Once, the Chinese had run the place – and the gold trade, the jewelry trade, in fact almost all the businesses. They were now gone without a trace but the whole area still had an unmistakable Chinese feel to it.

Our few days in Saigon were spent in similar searches for my past. Much had changed or was now gone – like my old USIS office. But on my last day, I decided to seek out my last home in Vietnam. I no longer remembered the street number on the main road, Cong Ly, but as we drove along I spotted a familiar building and the old villa at its side. I had arrived just in time; it was empty and about to be torn down. With a combination of sign language and a bit of remembered Vietnamese, I managed to explain to the gate guard that I had once lived there and just wanted to see it for a few minutes. He let me in and returned to his guard shack to read his newspaper, allowing me to wander around freely. I gazed up at the second-floor balcony and everything flooded back. It was like looking at an old photo, although now missing were two black dachshund faces peering down at me.

It was an eerie experience. I walked through the lofty lobby, now bare and crumbling, and up the staircase. The tiles had been stripped from the stairs and corridors – and from all the floors too, as I later discovered – and only the chipped concrete bases remained. The door to my flat stood open and I walked into a scene of utter desolation.

The flat had been crudely divided into two flats; down the center of the broad hallway was a raw, badly-laid brick wall, stopping just short of the door to the bathroom that lay between the front and back bedrooms. Obviously one tenant got the front part, the living room and a bedroom, and the other got the back bedroom and kitchen, and both shared the single bathroom. A second kitchen had been bricked into the corner of the long front balcony where once had been flowers, fish, birds, and palm trees, and rattan chairs had provided a peaceful bower for relaxing in the long evenings after work.

I looked at the door leading into the living room and there was the proof that I had once lived there: In the wooden door panel, now covered by a piece of plywood, was the little doggie door I had cut through it for my two dachshunds. (I wondered what the later and austere North Vietnamese tenants had thought of this small square hole; did they think, perhaps, that I had a very small child?) In my mind's eye, I saw again the lovely old flat and my two loyal companions, both long gone.

All the ceiling fans and light fixtures had been ripped out and the wiring dangled down. In the kitchen, the piping was all gone but the cabinets remained, warped and gaping open, their locks removed. Piles of rubbish lay everywhere. I kicked through it searching for something to take away, a souvenir of a part of my past life lived in this once-lovely old space. I finally unearthed a small lacquered sign in Vietnamese [now in my Washington hallway]. So long ago, so much lost. It all made me profoundly sad.

As I walked away, I looked back up at my old flat for the last time. For just a brief moment in my mind's eye I saw it just as it had looked when I lived there so long ago. It lifted my heart as I bade farewell to two small dogs peering out at me. With tears in my eyes, I walked away from my former life there.

The war-time drive to Dalat had been an adventure: I had then been driven through roadblocks, speeding up when we came to Viet Cong country, which then basically was everywhere in the countryside, although we didn't know that in the late 1960s. This trip was a totally different matter, but not necessarily better. While I remembered a six-hour drive through a lush countryside of small villages and unspoiled scenery, on this occasion it took us over three-quarters of our drive to find anything like that, and then only after we had turned off the main road and toward the mountains. For at least the first hundred miles on the main road to the north, it was now one long corridor of industry, roadside shops and urban sprawl of unbelievable ugliness. There was neither field nor farm nor any hint of beauty visible from our dense, spewing stream of traffic.

Our vision was not helped by the appalling miasma of pollution that hovered over the highway, indeed as far as the eye could see. I had originally hoped to stop by Bien Hoa and seek out my home overlooking our old Air Force base. As we crept along for over an hour in a gray haze, however, we decided to abandon that stop. I recalled how my old boss, John Paul Vann, used to boast that he could drive the twelve-mile Bien Hoa-Saigon stretch in seventeen minutes; with the city's "progress" it had taken us six to seven times longer.

After driving for several more hours, we began to catch glimpses of what I remembered: the lush Vietnamese countryside. The sky gradually became bluer and the fields more vividly green. However, the road itself was now lined by a sprawl of new housing – and indeed new villages – that had sprouted every few miles. In the past decade, the Vietnamese had obviously become more prosperous.

A word here about the uniquely Vietnamese style of housing. Housing is taxed on the width of the street frontage, thus most of the houses we saw, even the freestanding ones in the countryside, were four to six storeys tall but only one room wide. In Saigon and Hanoi they were even taller, and just as narrow. Although in Saigon these tall thin houses had adjoining buildings with common walls to reinforce them, standing alone in the countryside they looked like they would blow over in a strong wind; they certainly must have been more stable than they looked. They were often painted in vivid colors and as we drove farther into the countryside we began to note that almost every roof or balcony boasted a religious statue – in even more vivid colors. This was obviously Catholic country, as the Virgin Mary prevailed, often with a baby Jesus in arm, sometimes with a halo of Christmas lights. These country-dwellers were obviously deeply religious – or else a very persuasive religious statuary salesman had swept through the area. Every village through which we passed had a Catholic church also featuring massive, colorful statuary.

All this color was only eclipsed by the even more brilliant blooms that cascaded over walls, in flower boxes or in vacant bits of land along the road. Every flower and tree that we could name – and many that we could not – seemed to grow profusely here. This is the Vietnam that I remember, one of a profusion of flowers of intense colors and beauty, even then, amidst the destruction of war.

Luckily only the cities are cursed with the crippling pollution of a newly industrialized society. As we got closer to Dalat, we even dared to open the car windows to enjoy the smell of the clean, sweet air, a welcome relief from Saigon's air and from that we had been through on the drive. I continued to wax rhapsodic about the beauty of the old colonial hill station that awaited us at the end of our journey. Folly!

The air was still pure and the climate mild, but the old Dalat that I remembered appeared to be buried under a sea of new construction. Our old guidebook had described Dalat as being a town that hadn't changed much since the French departed. If, in the year 1934, someone had evacuated a province town somewhere in France and repopulated it with Vietnamese, this is what it would have looked like twenty years later." Alas, no more.

The streets were a beehive of activity with a rash of new tall and tasteless hotels. It seemed to us about as far from France as you could possibly get. Luckily, away from downtown and overlooking the lake, we found a stately old hotel built at the turn of the century – by the French, of course – the Palace Hotel. Here was the old Dalat – or, rather, the old France – that we sought. The long, low colonial building was set in a swath of greenery. Our room had a working fireplace, as evidenced by the lingering smell of hickory smoke, and shuttered French windows that opened onto a wide terrace. The room's ceilings were at least five meters high, the floors parquet, and the giant bathroom, although tastefully modernized, retained its original plumbing. Furnished in French antiques, our spacious, gracious room looked like a movie set (the film "Indochine" comes to mind).

As we began to explore, we also began to find other bits of France. We dined at a very French café, the De la Poste. A long walk to the top of a hill led us to a promising detour, a street of old villas. Most were in a very poor state but many were in the French style and all were charming. The more we wandered the more we found, although it never reached the point that would lead one to characterize today's Dalat as resembling a provincial town in France.

Still not villa-sated, the next day we decided to tour two famous old villas touted in our guidebook, one the former home of the Governor General of then-French Vietnam, now a guest house and for official receptions, and the other a 25-room villa that was once the summer palace of former emperor Bao Dai and is now a museum. Initially the fates were against us. The Governor General's residence was occupied by visiting officials, and Bao Dai's palace was "closed for repairs" – a formula that we recognized from China as one that could mean almost anything except that it was under repair.

The long and winding road that led to the latter did, however, hold promise. At the crest of the hill we spotted a fine old French provincial-style villa sitting in solitary splendor. The bored attendant in a small ticket booth at the driveway entrance seemed reluctant to sell us a ticket, but after an extended conversation our driver managed to buy us two – oddly enough, for the price of one. With such an investment we were dubious about what awaited us, but it turned out to be a jewel. We wandered around the villa's stunning hilltop setting. The overhanging eaves and attractive stonework of its exterior were beautifully designed and executed. The villa overlooked the town on one side and a distant valley on the other, a lovely setting for this country manor. Oh, how the French must have hated to give up their fine old villas in this gentle land.

On the road just below the villa, a different fate had befallen what appeared to have been a chapel and adjoining convent or school. In terrible condition, it appeared to be heavily tenanted by peasant squatters. It too was a complex of skillfully worked sandstone, once solid and stately, but no more. In its dereliction it was now a far cry from a serene convent.

In stark contrast to Dalat was the final city we visited, Hanoi. This was my first visit but I had high hopes for it, having heard of its fabled French architecture. I was not disappointed except, again, by the hovering pollution. Our suite had a balcony overlooking the magnificent old opera house; like Saigon's, it was a turn-of-the-century classic. We later purchased incredibly cheap tickets for a French music concert there and found the newly-renovated interior almost as lovely as the exterior.

The city's center of some forty square blocks appeared little updated from the previous century, but far more crowded. We spent several days walking its narrow, now motorbike-clogged, streets, peering into old shops and new art galleries and buying the occasional handicrafts or odd little objects not found elsewhere in Asia.

The most surprising to me was Hanoi's vibrant art scene. I was dazzled by the quality of the artwork on show there. An American friend was our introduction to the world of Vietnamese art and artists. She has created her stylish Art Vietnam Gallery in a traditional row house courtyard and gathered there the best of Vietnam's art. I found the level far higher – or at least more appealing to me personally – than anything I had seen anywhere in China. Touring the various galleries, I saw at least ten paintings that I would have bought in a heartbeat. Despite the depressed economy of Vietnam, however, its artwork was not cheap. Since every wall in all my homes is always so covered with artwork that there is no room for a single new piece, I was able to resist.

My short Vietnamese journey down memory lane ended all too soon. They say you can't go home again, but I did. Now my old home in Saigon is gone, along with much that I treasured. Vietnam will always remain for me, however, a country that I loved, and one where I was privileged to work for charismatic leaders and to serve with colleagues and friends in a war that we could not, did not, win.

Nonetheless, I would do it all over again.

THE QUIRKS OF FATE

AFTER I LEFT VIETNAM in 1974, my life veered off in a different direction and I lost touch with Sally for some thirty years. Then in 2005 she was in a quilt shop in Pennsylvania and noted that another customer was ordering a large quantity of quilting squares. When she commented on it, the lady replied that it was because she lived in China. Sally mentioned that she had once had a friend she heard was in China, and – a shot in the dark – asked the customer if she knew Tess Johnston.

'Oh yes,' the lady replied. 'In fact I just had lunch with her last week.' And so we met again, and our friendship continues to this day.

POSTSCRIPT

(OR WAS IT ALL WORTH IT?)

I AM OCCASIONALLY asked, as is anyone who spent time in Vietnam during the war, whether it was the right war fought wrong or the wrong war fought wrong. It's a good question.

During the war, when I returned to the U.S. on home leaves and then permanently in late 1974, I was occasionally challenged by some of my friends for having served in Vietnam, thus sanctioning the war. I often deflected it by saying 'my country right or wrong' and explained my role as a secretary to Vann and Colonel Wilson and later with USIS in Saigon. That usually sufficed, as the war at that point looked like it was winding down, which indeed is one of the reasons I had left.

On later Foreign Service assignments in Europe after the end of the war, interest in Vietnam died down, and indeed the war seemed to have been forgotten as it was eclipsed by other national and international events and crises. In recent years, however, with the publication of some first-person narratives by government officials, and in 2017 with a ten-part video series on the Vietnam War, interest has again flared up. I am now being asked again if I believe the war was justified.

Knowing what we have subsequently learned about the role that politics played in the war, I now believe that it was never justified. But that is hindsight. At the time, I went to Vietnam out of curiosity to see what it was really all about. Once there and caught up in the war, working for Vann and Colonel Wilson,

I initially believed with Vann that it could be won, or at least fought to a stalemate. And as it ground on, and after the withdrawal of most of the U.S. troops in 1972, I was more than ever convinced that it would keep winding down and come to just that – a stalemate. And I was wrong.

I also include here an assessment by a Foreign Service comrade with whom I served in Vietnam in the 1970s, the Lacy Wright of my narrative. It reflects my thoughts and is stated far more concisely, cogently and elegantly than I could ever do.

"We should not have gotten involved. Even if our side had won, the losses would have been more than American society could have borne, not to mention the dead and wounded on both of the Vietnamese sides.

That is not to say the South Vietnamese cause was unjust, or that the North Vietnamese communists deserved to win. The latter have successfully perpetuated the sleight of hand that has left most of the world believing that they were all along the legitimate rulers of the entire country, when, in fact, the South Vietnamese leadership in my view had an equal claim to legitimacy.

Both depended on foreign backing. By 1956, both were independent countries – North Vietnam because it had defeated the French in a long bloody war, and South Vietnam because it had negotiated hard with the French to force the French to acknowledge its independence. What differentiated the two was that North Vietnam was far more brutal, having killed off a number of the non-Communist pretenders to power, was fanatically driven under charismatic leadership, created a large and battle-hardened military, and, with the essential backing of the Soviets and Chinese, outlasted the Americans.

Might, in other words, made right."

A WAR AWAY

Courtesy of Lacy A. Wright, Jr., former FSO in Vietnam, who exited off the Embassy roof on that last night

ABOUT THE AUTHOR

TESS JOHNSTON is a native of Virginia and her academic background includes a M.A. from the University of Virginia, where she subsequently taught. She has served abroad for more than half a century, including seven years in East and West Berlin and more than 40 years in Asia, 33 in Shanghai and seven in Vietnam (1967-74). Tess moved to Shanghai in 1981 to work at the US Consulate General and in 1996, after over 30 years in the Foreign Service, retired and stayed on until her 2016 repatriation. She now writes, researches and lectures in Washington, DC. She and her co-author, photographer Deke Erh (Er Donqiang), have published more than twenty books, including 10 volumes on Western architecture and the expatriate experience in old China.

She can be contacted at tessinshanghai@yahoo.com